MW00477267

OKANOGAN
NF

Okanogan

Ferry

Kettle River Range

COLVILLE
NF

COLVILLE
NF

LITTLE PEND
OREILLE
NWR

Pend
Oreille

Priest
Lake

Methow R.

Okanogan R.

Kettle R.

Columbia R.

Pend Oreille R.

• Winthrop

LAKE CHELAN
NRA

Okanogan •

COLVILLE
INDIAN
RESERVATION

Colville •

LAKE
ROOSEVELT
NRA

Calispell Peak ▲
6,861

KANIKSU
NF

Newport •

WENATCHEE
NF

Chelan

*Lake
Chelan*

Douglas

Columbia R.

Sanpoil R.

Grand
Coulee

*Franklin D.
Roosevelt Lake*

Stevens

SPOKANE
INDIAN
RESERVATION

*Long
Lake*

Spokane R.

◉ **Spokane**

Wenatchee R.

*Waterville
Plateau*

*Banks
Lake*

Davenport •

Lincoln

Spokane

Wenatchee •

Grant

Douglas

Crab Cr.

TURNBULL
NWR

Kittitas

*Potholes
Reservoir*

• Moses
Lake

Ritzville •

*Sprague
Lake*

*Rock
Lake*

• Ellensburg

Vantage •

COLUMBIA
NWR

Adams

Whitman

Palouse R.

Pullman •

◉ **Yakima**

SADDLE
MOUNTAIN
NWR

• Othello

Columbia

Basin

Yakima R.

Columbia R.

Franklin

Snake R.

Garfield

Snake R.

Yakima

Benton

JUNIPER DUNES
WILDERNESS

*Lake
Sacajawea*

Columbia

Asotin

Sunnyside •

TOPPENISH NWR

Richland •

Pasco •

MCNARY
NWR

Walla Walla

*Blue
Mountains*

Diamond Peak
▲ 4,659

YAKAMA
INDIAN
RESERVATION

◉ **Kennewick**

Walla •
Walla

UMATILLA
NF

Grande Ronde R.

Klickitat

UMATILLA
NWR

Columbia R.

OREGON

IDAHO

American Birding Association
Field Guide to Birds
of Washington

American Birding Association

Field Guide

to Birds of

Washington

Dennis Paulson

PHOTOGRAPHS BY
Brian E. Small
and Others

Scott & Nix, Inc.
NEW YORK

Contents

vii *American Birding*
Association Mission
Statement
AND *Code of Ethics*

xi *Foreword*
BY JEFFREY A. GORDON, PRESIDENT,
AMERICAN BIRDING ASSOCIATION

xiii *Introduction*
BIRDS OF WASHINGTON *xiii*

THE SCOPE OF THIS GUIDE *xvi*

WASHINGTON'S BIRDING
REGIONS *xvii*

THE BIRDING YEAR IN
WASHINGTON *xxi*

PARTS OF A BIRD *xxvi*

IDENTIFYING BIRDS *xxix*

ATTRACTING BIRDS *xxxi*

SPECIES ACCOUNTS *xxxi*

RESOURCES FOR WASHINGTON
BIRDERS *xxxii*

2 Geese
8 Swans
10 Ducks
38 Quails
40 Chukar
41 Partridge
42 Pheasant
43 Grouse
51 Turkey
52 Grebes
58 Pigeons
60 Doves
62 Nightjars
64 Swifts
67 Hummingbirds

71 Rails
74 Crane
75 Shorebirds
112 Jaegers
115 Alcids
122 Gulls
134 Terns
139 Loons
142 Albatross
143 Petrels
147 Cormorants
150 Pelicans
152 Herons
157 Vulture
158 Hawks
172 Owls
186 Kingfisher
187 Woodpeckers
199 Falcons
203 Flycatchers
214 Shrikes
216 Vireos
220 Corvids
227 Lark
228 Swallows
235 Chickadees
239 Bushtit
240 Nuthatches
243 Creeper
244 Wrens
250 Dipper
251 Kinglets
253 Thrushes
261 Mimids
263 Starling
264 Waxwings
266 House Sparrow

267 Pipit

268 Finches

280 Longspur

281 Snow Bunting

282 Towhees

284 Sparrows

300 Chat

301 Icterids

311 Warblers

324 Tanager

325 Grosbeak

326 Bunting

328 *Acknowledgments*

329 *Image Credits*

330 *Official Washington
Ornithological Society
Checklist of Washington
Birds*

339 *Species Index*

The American Birding Association inspires all people to enjoy and protect wild birds.

The ABA represents the North American birding community and supports birders through publications, conferences, workshops, events, partnerships, and networks.

The ABA's education programs promote birding skills, ornithological knowledge, and the development of and implementation of a conservation ethic.

The ABA encourages birders to apply their skills to help conserve birds and their habitats, and we represent the interests of birders in planning and legislative arenas.

We welcome all birders as members.

**THE AMERICAN BIRDING ASSOCIATION
CODE OF ETHICS V. 2.1, NOVEMBER 2019**

1. Respect and promote birds and their environment.

(a) Support the conservation of birds and their habitats. Engage in and promote bird-friendly practices whenever possible, such as keeping cats and other domestic animals indoors or controlled, acting to prevent window strikes, maintaining safe feeding stations, landscaping with native plants, drinking shade-grown coffee, and advocating for conservation policies. Be mindful of any negative environmental impacts of your activities, including contributing to climate change. Reduce or offset such impacts as much as you are able.

(b) Avoid stressing birds or exposing them to danger. Be particularly cautious around active nests and nesting colonies, roosts, display sites, and feeding sites. Limit the use of recordings and other audio methods of attracting birds, particularly in heavily birded areas, for species that are rare in the area, and for species that are threatened or endangered. Always exercise caution and restraint when photographing, recording, or otherwise approaching birds.

(c) Always minimize habitat disturbance. Consider the benefits of staying on trails, preserving snags, and similar practices. 2. Respect and promote the birding community and its individual members.

(a) Be an exemplary ethical role model by following this Code and leading by example. Always bird and report with honesty and integrity.

(b) Respect the interests, rights, and skill levels of fellow birders, as well as people participating in other outdoor activities. Freely share your knowledge and experience and be especially helpful to beginning birders.

(c) Share bird observations freely, provided such reporting would not violate other sections of this Code, as birders, ornithologists, and conservationists derive considerable benefit from publicly available bird sightings.

(d) Approach instances of perceived unethical birding behavior with sensitivity and respect; try to resolve the matter in a positive manner, keeping in mind that perspectives vary. Use the situation as an opportunity to teach by example and to introduce more people to this Code.

(e) In group birding situations, promote knowledge by everyone in the group of the practices in this Code and ensure that the group does not unduly interfere with others using the same area.

3. Respect and promote the law and the rights of others.

(a) Never enter private property without the landowner's permission. Respect the interests of and interact positively with people living in the area where you are birding.

(b) Familiarize yourself with and follow all laws, rules, and
regulations governing activities at your birding location.
In particular, be aware of regulations related to birds,
such as disturbance of protected nesting areas or
sensitive habitats, and the use of audio or food lures.

▸ Birding should be fun and help build a better future for
birds, for birders, and for all people

▸ Birds and birding opportunities are shared resources that
should be open and accessible to all

▸ Birders should always give back more than they take

Everyone who enjoys birds and birding must always
respect wildlife, its environment, and the rights of others.
The ABA Code of Ethics should be read, followed, and
shared by all birders.

Please follow this code and distribute and teach it to others.

The American Birding Association's Code of Birding Ethics
may be freely reproduced for distribution/dissemination.
An electronic version may be found at www.aba.org/aba-code-
of-birding-ethics/.

Foreword

Washington is a wondrous place for birding, offering a wealth of prime habitats for birds and outstanding opportunities for birders of all levels.

Like all the guides in this series, this book can help you do whatever you want with birding. Perhaps you enjoy birds a few days a year in your yard or local park and just want to know a little more about them and to know some of their names. Or maybe you want to dive deeper and really get familiar with the hundreds of amazing birds that call Washington home for part or all of each year. Our aim is to meet you where you are and give you useful, reliable information and insight into birds and birding.

Author Dennis Paulson is the perfect guide for those wanting to explore the birds of Washington. You're in very good hands with him. The gorgeous photography by Brian E. Small and others will not only aid your identifications—it will inspire you to get out and see more of these beautiful and fascinating creatures for yourself.

I invite you to visit the American Birding Association website (aba.org), where you'll find a wealth of free resources and ways to connect with the birding community that will also help you get the most from your birding in Washington and beyond. Please consider becoming an ABA member yourself—one of the best parts of birding is joining a community of fun, passionate people.

Now get on out there! Enjoy this book. Enjoy Washington. And most of all, enjoy birding!

Good birding,

Jeffrey A Gordon

Jeffrey A. Gordon, *President*
American Birding Association

Birds of Washington

It may be the smallest state in the West, but Washington has all the features it needs to be a superlative place for birds and birdwatchers. It has water in abundance, with over 3,000 miles of saltwater shoreline. These waters are among the most productive in the country, with birds coming to our outer coast and protected waters in great numbers from all directions. No other state has a higher diversity of migrant and wintering seabirds than we do right here in Washington. Offshore, Northern Fulmars from the Bering Sea mix with Sooty Shearwaters from New Zealand.

There are also about 8,000 lakes and innumerable ponds, streams, rivers, and other wetlands spread across the state, and there are many breeding freshwater birds as well, especially in the open and wooded lakes of the Columbia Basin and northeast corner. The state also abounds with waterbird migrants spring and fall, and many of them winter where the water remains unfrozen. Nesting species includes Common Loons and Buffleheads from the north and Black-necked Stilts and Forster's Terns from the south. Waterfowl are as diverse and abundant in Washington as in any of the Lower 48 states.

The lovely thistle-eating American Goldfinch was named Washington's state bird in 1951.

And we have mountains. The Cascades divide the state into a western and eastern half, with volcanic peaks attaining elevations of greater than 10,000 feet and glacier-mantled Mount Rainier reaching 14,410 feet. The western slopes of these mountains capture much of the moisture coming from the Pacific on southwest winds. So, looking for ptarmigans and rosy-finches high on Rainier, you could look one way and see vast expanses of wet forest on Washington's westside, with breeding Sooty Grouse, Varied Thrushes, and Townsend's Warblers.

Turning around to the east, you would view more forests, but the climate becomes drier and drier on the east slopes of the Cascades on Washington's eastside, as the mountains them-selves have captured the moisture coming from the Pacific. Here there are Mountain Chickadees and Cassin's Finches. As the mountainsides slope ever downward to the east, the view would be of drier, more open country as far as the eye can see until the land slopes upward again into forested mountains.

The pure tones of the Varied Thrush ring from dense conifer forests in Washington's mountains.

Look for cacti, horned lizards, rattlesnakes, and jackrabbits in Washington's very dry landscapes, with annual rainfall no more than seven inches in the lower parts of the Columbia Basin, Here you can find Sage Thrashers and Loggerhead Shrikes and numerous sparrow species in the sagebrush along with them, as well as Prairie Falcons, Say's Phoebes, and Rock Wrens nesting in the dry cliffs.

Other mountain ranges include the isolated Olympics in the west and the Blue Mountains in the Southeast. And from Okanogan County eastward, the extensive Northeastern Highlands extend into the state as outliers of the Rocky Mountains, with Spruce Grouse, Boreal Chickadees, and Pine Grosbeaks. Each of these ranges has its own birds, and in a study of the diversity of breeding birds in North America, the northeast corner of Washington turned out to have species numbers not far below the highest in southern Arizona!

Rock Wrens are favorites of birders because of the towering basalt cliffs they inhabit in the Columbia Basin.

The Scope of this Guide

A complete list of the 518 bird species known to have occurred in Washington State is on page 330. This guide covers 308 of them, including all of the species a birder is reasonably likely to encounter in an active year of birding across the state, including at least one offshore boat trip.

All of Washington's breeding species are included except Northern Bobwhite, a very local introduced species; White-faced Ibis and Black Phoebe, rare visitors that have bred once; and White-tailed Kite, Red-shouldered Hawk, Northern Hawk Owl, Least Flycatcher, Northern Mockingbird, and Clay-colored and Black-throated Sparrows, all of uncertain status as Washington breeders.

In addition to the breeders, this book also includes all migrant and wintering birds that are common enough for an active birder to expect to see in the course of a year with regular time spent in the field. Pelagic species—birds of the open ocean—are included only if they are likely to be seen on a single fall trip thirty miles out into the Pacific.

Brants migrate from the Arctic in flocks to winter in Washington's large bays and estuaries.

Many species that occur only rarely each year are not included. Extreme rarities, categorized as "casual" or "accidental" in occurrence, are also excluded. Until recently, it was extremely unlikely that a beginning birder (or any birder) would have been so fortunate as to see a bird in those cateories. Now, with eBird, birding listservs, and Facebook groups, every rarity is immediately publicized and is potentially accessible to anyone who wants to hop in the car and make a beeline for the spot.

Washington's Birding Regions

OUTER COAST

Extending from Cape Flattery to the mouth of the Columbia River, this region includes the very large inlets of Grays Harbor and Willapa Bay. From Point Grenville north, the coast is rocky, with many small islands that serve as nesting sites for seabirds such as Brandt's Cormorants, Tufted Puffins, and Black Oystercatchers. From Point Grenville south, it is all sand beaches. Offshore waters support many additional birds that rarely come within sight of land.

The many islands on Washington's coast provide nesting habitat for Black Oystercatchers, and their bright red bills and loud calls make them hard to miss.

SALISH SEA

This huge area of water, with a long and varied shoreline, reaches from the mouth of the Strait of Juan de Fuca east to Admiralty Inlet and south through Puget Sound and the Hood Canal. It also extends north along Whidbey Island and through the San Juan Islands to the Canadian border. These waters are home to many of the same birds that dwell along the outer coast, but many more find the sheltered channels and bays attractive. Most of the waterfowl wintering in the state can be found here. Smaller islands are used as nest sites by colonial seabirds such as Pelagic Cormorants and Glaucous-winged Gulls.

WESTERN LOWLANDS

The Puget Trough, with most of the major Washington cities, makes up a large part of the western lowlands, but this region also includes the less populated southwest corner of the state, where low hills rise above the lowlands. Originally, wet forests of western hemlock, western red cedar, and Douglas-fir covered this entire area. Even after many years of logging and settlement, most of the forest birds, including Hutton's Vireos, Chestnut-backed Chickadees, and Swainson's Thrushes, still thrive throughout the area. Scattered patches of oak savanna support birds of drier areas, such as House Wrens and Chipping Sparrows.

Red-breasted Nuthatches are among the numerous bird species that inhabit the dense forests of the western Washington lowlands.

HIGH CASCADES

Above about 3,000 feet, the western slopes of the Cascades are home to a high-mountain flora and fauna. As elevation increases, the dominant conifers change from western hemlock to mountain hemlock and from silver fir to subalpine fir. Hermit Thrushes and Pine Grosbeaks breed here. Clark's Nutcrackers and American Pipits inhabit the subalpine parkland, and Gray-crowned Rosy-Finches and White-tailed Ptarmigan live at the highest elevations.

EASTSIDE FORESTS

From the Cascade crest downward to the east, the climate becomes drier and drier. Western larch and Douglas-fir replace the dense conifers of the higher mountain forests and provide habitat for Williamson's Sapsuckers and Cassin's Finches. Lower down, White-headed Woodpeckers, Gray Flycatchers, and Pygmy Nuthatches inhabit even more open ponderosa pine forests. Corridors of broadleaf trees and shrubs provide habitat for Red-naped Sapsuckers, Yellow Warblers, and Black-headed Grosbeaks. A similar mixture of conifer and broadleaf forests occurs all over the other highland areas to the east, with similar assemblages of birds.

Clark's Nutcrackers can be seen at close range at visitor centers in the national parks of the Cascade Mountains.

COLUMBIA PLATEAU

As the climate gets drier and drier east of the mountains, grassland replaces pines, and Horned Larks, Vesper Sparrows, and Western Meadowlarks become the predominant species. Eventually, at the lowest altitudes on the plateau, the grassland gives way to shrub steppe. The birds here are of southern origin, including Burrowing Owls, Sage Thrashers, and Sagebrush Sparrows. The open alkaline lakes of the plateau feature Western and Clark's Grebes, many waterfowl species, avocets and stilts, and breeding colonies of cormorants, herons, gulls, and terns.

NORTHEASTERN HIGHLANDS

As in the Cascades, plants and animals are regularly replaced by other species with increasing elevation: Spruce Grouse replace Dusky Grouse, and Boreal Chickadees replace Mountain Chickadees. Engelmann spruce and lodgepole pine are among the dominant trees high in the mountains. At lower elevations, especially in stands of birches and aspens, more typically eastern birds such as Veeries, Gray Catbirds, American Redstarts, and Northern Waterthrushes are common.

American Redstarts are among the birds of eastern origin in the deciduous groves of the state's northeast corner.

BLUE MOUNTAINS

This forested mountain range, with affinities to the Rockies, is Washington's only breeding area for Green-tailed Towhees. This region also features many birds of montane conifer forest, such as Northern Goshawks, Calliope Hummingbirds, and Townsend's Solitaires.

The Birding Year in Washington

January is an exciting time. Some birders can't wait to get up on the first day, midnight celebrations notwithstanding, to see their first bird of the year and share it with friends on social media. If northern birds such as Snowy Owls or redpolls have invaded the state for the winter, now is the time to seek them out. Visit the Skagit County flats and keep your eyes peeled for wintering hawks, falcons, and Short-eared Owls. Okanogan and Douglas Counties are favorites among Seattle birders for looking for wintering species such as Snow Buntings and redpolls, even Gyrfalcons and Snowy Owls.

Short-eared Owls hunt voles in winter in the farmlands of western Washington.

February is less rainy than the three months before, and the days are getting longer. All the winter birds are still present, hunting season is over and waterfowl are less spooky, and at the end of the month a few migrants even arrive, including Rufous Hummingbirds and Tree and Violet-green Swallows. This is the month to visit the flats of Skagit County, when the Snow Geese feed right along the roads, or to look for Gray-crowned Rosy-Finches along the Columbia River near Vantage.

March is a good time to visit birding spots you didn't hit in January or February, as you never know what you might have missed. All the wintering seabirds and shorebirds are still around; places like Ediz Hook and Semiahmoo Spit are usually hotspots at this season. In the sagebrush country, bluebirds and Sagebrush Sparrows are arriving and in full song, as are Western Meadowlarks and Horned Larks.

April is when birds of all kinds begin to breed. Singing picks up, and many songbirds that wintered in the Southwest are arriving and setting up territories. Shorebird numbers are increasing daily on the outer coast. All the winter waterfowl are still around, and Blue-winged and Cinnamon Teal are arriving to join them. This is the month to see courtship and mating in our many waterfowl species.

Ruddy Turnstones are among the many shorebird species that stop to feed along the outer coast every spring.

May is the month of massive arrivals, when the great majority of the songbirds that have wintered to our south appear on their breeding territories. Anywhere is a good place to be in May if you like seeing birds and listening to their songs. At the same time, shorebird migration is in full swing at the coast, and thousands are feeding and roosting at Bottle Beach State Park. Seabirds that have wintered in California, such as Pacific and Red-throated Loons and scoters, are moving up the coast by the hundreds, to be seen from the jetties on either side of Grays Harbor.

June is the month for you if you love hearing the songs of birds. Just about all the songbirds are singing now, but the chorus will dwindle as the month goes on, so you should spend as much time out listening as you can. Eastern Washington, with its variety of habitats and higher breeding-bird diversity, is the place to be. From the shrub steppe and cliffs of Frenchman Coulee through cottonwood-lined Umtanum Canyon, up through the pines of Cle Elum and the Wenas Creek region to the spruce and fir forests at Blewett Pass, there are birds everywhere. A birding trip every weekend wouldn't be too much, even one to the coast to see the first Sooty Shearwaters and Heermann's Gulls coming up from the south.

Lazuli Buntings sing from shrubby hillsides throughout the open country east of the Cascades.

With singing largely over, *July* is the time to look for all the young birds that have fledged, an opportunity to learn juvenile plumages by seeing the young in the company of their more distinctively marked parents. It's also time to think about shorebirds again, as they return by the thousands from their arctic and subarctic breeding grounds. Most are on the coast, but fresh water habitats also have potential. Check Bottle Beach again, but look for drying-up ponds and reservoirs east of the Cascades, for example Lind Coulee.

In *August*, shorebird aficionados review their knowledge of plumages, as this is when the juveniles arrive from the breeding grounds, a month after their parents. Songbird migration gets in full swing, as some species head south as soon as their young fledge; others hang around longer and undergo their autumn molt before migrating. The key to finding migrants is to look everywhere, even in city parks and your backyard.

September features migrants everywhere, shorebirds and dabbling ducks streaming down the coast, hawks over the mountain ridges, and a great variety of songbirds in the thickets, especially in oases and riparian woodland east of the Cascades. Check out the beaches and estuaries of Grays Harbor; take a trip to Sunrise on Mount Rainier or participate in a hawk watch at Cooper Ridge; and head to Washtucna or

Wilson's Warblers are everywhere in Washington during spring and fall migration.

one of the other oases in the Columbia Basin where migrants accumulate, sometimes with rarities among them.

October is a chance to enjoy later migrants of all kinds. Leaves may have turned color and drifted to the ground, but there are still birds in the trees. Birds such as sparrows that subsist on seeds hang around later than the insect-eating warblers and flycatchers. Many of the birds that come from the north first arrive in late September but peak in October, so it is still worth paying a return visit to the same good birding spots.

November is the rainiest month in many parts of the state, making it a good time to stay inside and catch up on your field notes. But not every day is wet, so check the forecast. This is when many diving ducks are forced southward by the freeze-up of lakes in Alaska and western Canada. Many birders find time to spend a few days at Neah Bay, at the northwest tip of the state, where more rarities may show up in a day than most other parts of the state see in a year. Prepare for stormy weather, though.

December is the month for Christmas Bird Counts. Participating in one or more enhances your knowledge and brings you together with other birders to exchange stories. And you will have the satisfaction of contributing to a very important citizen science project that has been going on for more than a century.

American Kestrels hunt from the air for insects in summer and rodents in winter.

The Parts of a Bird

The following illustrations with captions point out the prominent aspects of five major groups of birds.

secondaries · spectacles · crown · wing bars · primaries · tail · throat · coverts · breast · belly · undertail coverts

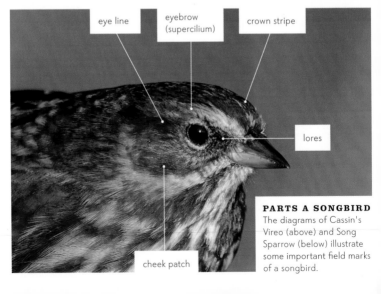

eye line · eyebrow (supercilium) · crown stripe · lores · cheek patch

PARTS A SONGBIRD
The diagrams of Cassin's Vireo (above) and Song Sparrow (below) illustrate some important field marks of a songbird.

crown

forehead

nape

throat

back

neck

breast

belly

PARTS OF A GULL
This adult Ring-billed
Gull shares many aspects
with other gulls.

legs

wing tip

tail

toes

tail

tertials

scapulars

back

bill

undertail coverts

flank

neck

breast

PARTS OF A DUCK
This adult male Northern Pintail shows major
parts of a duck's body as it rests on the water.

PARTS OF A SHOREBIRD
This diagram of an adult Black-bellied Plover shows some of the major features of a shorebird.

primaries

eyebrow (supercilium)

secondaries

axillars

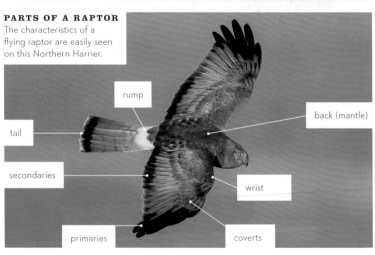

PARTS OF A RAPTOR
The characteristics of a flying raptor are easily seen on this Northern Harrier.

rump

back (mantle)

tail

secondaries

wrist

primaries

coverts

Identifying Birds

Identifying birds can be as easy as seeing a bird well and looking through the pages of a field guide to match the bird with an illustration. This works well for such nearly unmistakable birds as a magpie or an adult Bald Eagle. But other cases may require a bit more effort.

A good series of words to remember is Size, Shape, Pattern, and Color. Most birds don't perch near rulers, but they do perch on fence posts, branches, and twigs, or next to objects on the ground that are of known size or could even be measured after the observation. You are fortunate if your bird is near another bird that you have already identified, as you can look up their comparative sizes.

Shape is mostly determined by relative tail length. A "slender" bird is often considered so just because it has a long tail. A bird of the same weight with a short tail might be called "dumpy" or "chubby."

A female Wood Duck can be identified by her white eye patch, puffy crest, and glint of blue in the wing.

We usually notice color first when we see an unknown bird, but the pattern of a bird is very important, independent of those colors. Does it have an eye line? An eye ring? Wing bars? A contrasting head or breast pattern? Pale edges on the tail? Review the photos of bird anatomy to become familiar with the terms used for all of these "field marks."

Color differences in birds are often subtle. Browse through the photos of flycatchers, sandpipers, and sparrows to note some of these subtle differences in grays and browns and buffs and yellows.

An important step in learning about birds is to also learn about their environment. Knowing how to identify the common trees and other plants in your area can be a great advantage, as certain birds are attracted to certain plants. There is also a benefit in knowing your trees when someone says, "Look at that falcon in the top of the Sitka spruce."

A Ruby-crowned Kinglet becomes easy to identify when a male flashes his crest.

Attracting Birds

Many birds can be attracted to your yard if it provides appropriate habitat and food. You can increase your chances by maintaining a bird feeder. Millet seeds are favored by many small seed-eating birds. Sunflower seeds come with or without shells; without shells means there will be no mess under your feeders. Thistle (niger) seed attracts goldfinches and siskins.

Suet can attract woodpeckers, wintering warblers, and kinglets. Chickadees, nuthatches, jays, flickers, and wrens are happy with both seeds and suet. Bark butter, a mixture of suet and peanut butter, is also very popular with birds. And there are four species of hummingbirds in Washington that come to feeders to drink sugar water, including Anna's, present all winter.

Birds are also attracted to water in from bird baths and fountains. A trickling fountain will bring migrants down from the trees in spring and fall, birds you might never see in your yard otherwise.

Species Accounts

The common and scientific names of each species are followed by indications of average length (L) and wingspan (WS). Remember that these measurements are averages, and species may vary in size, especially when one sex is larger than the other. Note also that the length of a bird's tail affects its total length; a long-tailed bird may in fact weigh less than another bird with a shorter tail.

The text account indicates where and when a species is usually present in the state. Many birds are too common and widespread to require the mention of individual localities, but some species are of sufficiently limited distribution that favored localities can be named. Details that are useful for identification are indicated in the photo captions; this can be augmented by further description in the text, especially of characteristic behavior.

"West," "westside," "east," and "eastside" refer to the western and eastern halves of Washington, divided by the Cascade Mountains. The eastside is also called the interior. Common abbreviations are NWR, National Wildlife Refuge; SP - State Park; WA - Wildlife Area.

Descriptions of occurrence refer to the times and places a species is most likely to be seen. Coastal shorebirds may rarely turn up in the interior, and Columbia Basin sparrows might be seen somewhere in the western lowlands, but unless these are regular occurrences, they are usually not mentioned in the text. Similarly, migrants associated with forested habitats might turn up occasionally in the Columbia Basin.

When dates of occurrence are given as months (for example, July–August), birds are present through the entire months. If most individuals arrive or leave during a month, that is indicated. Birds don't follow strict timetables, and they may occur slightly outside of the time spans given here.

The photos are typical of each species. In most cases, they do not show all the possible plumages of the bird that might be seen in Washington, especially juveniles, nonbreeding plumages of species that are present only as breeders, and breeding plumages of species that are present only as nonbreeders.

For the most part, the vocalizations of birds rarely heard calling or singing in Washington are not described. Songs vary geographically, and the descriptions here refer to the way a bird typically sounds in Washington. Furthermore, most birds have many more vocalizations than are described.

Resources for Washington Birders

BOOKS

Birds of Washington. Eds. Terence M. Wahl, Bill Tweit, and Steven G. Mlodinow. Oregon State University Press. 2005.

A Birder's Guide to Washington, 2nd edition. Ed. Jane Hadley. American Birding Association. 2015.

Birds of the Pacific Northwest: A Photographic Guide. Tom Aversa, Richard Cannings, and Hal Opperman. University of Washington Press. 2016.

Birds of the Pacific Northwest. John Shewey and Tim Blount. Timber Press. 2017.

Birds of the Puget Sound Region, Coast to Cascades. Dennis Paulson, Bob Morse, Tom Aversa, and Hal Opperman. R. W. Morse Company 2016.

Of the field guides covering all the birds of North America, these are recommended:

The Sibley Guide to Birds, 2nd edition. David Sibley. Knopf. 2014.

National Geographic Field Guide to the Birds of North America, 7th edition. Jon Dunn and Jonathan Alderfer. National Geographic Society. 2017.

OTHER RESOURCES

Audubon Washington (wa.audubon.org), the regional representative of the National Audubon Society, spearheads bird conservation efforts in the state. The website includes links to local Audubon chapters.

BirdWeb (birdweb.org/birdweb/), created by Seattle Audubon Society, provides further information about Washington's birds.

Tweeters (mailman11.u.washington.edu/mailman/listinfo/tweeters) is a listserv for Washington birders to report sightings and ask and answer questions about birds.

eBird (ebird.org/home) is a citizenscience project gathering bird sightings from all over the world. eBird is of great value in learning about the distribution and seasonal occurrence of birds in Washington.

The eBird Dashboard (birdingwashington.info/dashboard/wa/) is a good way to get information about local bird sightings.

American Birding Association

Field Guide to
Birds of Washington

Snow Goose

Anser caerulescens

L 28" | **WS** 53"

Tens of thousands of Snow Geese come from Siberia's Wrangel Island to winter on the agricultural lands of the lower Skagit and Samish Rivers from October to April, filling the sky like an avian blizzard. They feed on bulrush rhizomes in Skagit Bay, then, after hunting season, move to agricultural fields to graze. This population is increasing rapidly, and flocks are seen far and wide, including thousands in the interior, where they feed on cropland. Perhaps the most vocal of all waterfowl, flocks call incessantly with one- or two-syllable high-pitched, nasal honks, noisy but musical.

Medium-sized white goose with black wing tips and black "grinning patch" on bill. Immature mostly gray, with dark bill and legs and all flight feathers dark; begins to molt to white over the winter.

Greater White-fronted Goose
Anser albifrons

L 28" | **WS** 53"

These geese are common in the state as coastal migrants April–May and again September–November, when flock after flock passes by with Cackling and Canada Geese, heading to and from arctic breeding grounds. They are less common in the east, but large numbers have turned up repeatedly in several places including McNary NWR; numbers are apparently still increasing. Like our other migratory geese, they stop briefly to graze and then move on. Very few, often single birds, remain over the winter. Flocks give two- or three-syllable calls, more like laughing than honking.

Medium-sized brown goose with white patch around pinkish to orange bill, black markings on underparts, and orange legs. Immature lacks white around bill and black markings below. Similar domestic Greylag Goose has pink legs.

Brant

Branta bernicla

L 25"　**WS** 42"

Our only seagoing geese, Brant are common winterers from
late October to early May in large bays on both the outer coast
and Salish Sea. They are especially conspicuous in April, as
they migrate through Puget Sound to feed on eelgrass and sea
lettuce, usually at or near the shore. Most Brant in Washington
are black-bellied migrants from western Alaska, while gray-
bellied birds from the central Canadian Arctic predominate
around Padilla Bay. A very few are seen in migration on inland
lakes on both sides of the state. Calls throaty *arrnhh arrnhh*,
hoarser and less musical than other geese.

Small, mostly very dark marine
goose with white neck ring.
White rear end almost covering
dark tail is prominent in flight.

Cackling Goose

Branta hutchinsii

L 25" | **WS** 43"

Cackling Geese are common coastal migrants and increasingly common wintering birds in westside lowlands. Ridgefield and Nisqually NWRs are notable for large flocks, but they also wander well outside the refuges to graze on open land, sometimes with other geese. Small, dark Aleutian breeders are uncommon coastal migrants on the way to their California wintering grounds. Note that the largest Cackling Geese are about the size of the smallest Canada Geese, posing an identification challenge. Flocks make a characteristic high-pitched yelping sound.

Like a small Canada Goose with a tiny bill. Most are very small and rather dark-breasted. Some are larger and paler, but still identifiable by the rather small bill. High-pitched calls distinctive.

Canada Goose

Branta canadensis

L 40" | **WS** 55"

This large, common goose is an example of a bird that has adapted perhaps too well to human activities. Steadily increasing in the state for decades, flocks feed and defecate on the expansive lawns of city parks and honk like passing cars. Washington's resident population nests just about everywhere there is open water; its numbers are augmented by thousands of migrants from the Arctic, many of which winter from October to April on Columbia Basin lakes and feed in surrounding farmlands. Flocks of Dusky Canada Geese, an Alaskan population of conservation concern, winter in the southwest corner of the state.

Resident birds large; brown with long black neck and white chin patch.

Migrants from the Arctic
considerably smaller and
shorter-necked.
U-shaped white rump
patch prominent in flight
on all Canada Geese.

Wintering Dusky
Canada Goose
from Alaska with
a very dark body.

Trumpeter Swan

Cygnus buccinator

L 60" | **WS** 80"

These magnificent white birds, the largest by weight in North America, are a conservation success story. Almost gone from Washington 50 years ago, they are now common in the northwest counties from Whatcom to Snohomish and in small numbers everywhere else in the west, where they feed on aquatic plants, waste grain, and potatoes. Largest numbers are present November–March. Smaller numbers migrate through the eastside, stopping at McNary and Umatilla NWRs and the Grand Coulee lakes, but they are possible anywhere. The calls sound like single low notes from a toy trumpet.

Very large white waterfowl. Black bill relatively wide at eye. Bill meets feathers of face in a diagonal line. Often rests with base of neck on back. Immature gray through first winter.

Tundra Swan

Cygnus columbianus

L 52" | **WS** 66"

Tundra Swans migrate widely through the state and winter commonly October–April in the same northwest quadrant as the Trumpeter; they also winter commonly along the Lower Columbia River. Ridgefield and Steigerwald NWRs have large numbers. East of the Cascades, they are common spring migrants at wetlands such as Calispell Lake and on flooded fields in the Columbia Basin. Distant flocks are distinguished from Trumpeters by the paler immatures and by their loud, musical, sonorous calls.

Large white waterfowl. Most have yellow spot at bill base. Those without yellow spot distinguished by black of bill pinched in at eye. Line between rear edge of bill and face feathers more vertical than in Trumpeter. Often rests with neck curved. Immatures turn white during first winter.

Wood Duck

Aix sponsa

L 18.5" | **WS** 30"

Very rare a century ago, the Wood Duck is now a common
summer resident west and less common east. As the populations continue to increase, more are wintering in the state,
taking advantage of food handouts, especially at urban lakes.
Nesting in tree holes and nest boxes, this is our only duck that
commonly perches in trees. Wood ducks were restricted to
wooded lakes before nest boxes were provided at more open
sites. Female Wood Ducks give a loud *whoooeeek* in flight.

Male's colorful head with bushy
crest distinctive; iridescent dark
blue wings. Tail longer than other
dabbling ducks (ducks that feed
on the surface). Juvenile male
brown, with face pattern like adult.

Female shaped like male, with bushy
head, but big white eyepatch and throat
contrast with gray head, light brown
body. Wings with iridescent blue
primaries and white rear edge as in male.

Northern Shoveler

Spatula clypeata

L 19" | **WS** 30"

Fairly common breeders and very common migrants and winter visitors, Northern Shovelers are found throughout the state on fresh water and, less commonly, shallow estuaries. These are the typical ducks of sewage ponds, for example, at Hoquiam and Everett. Individuals and small groups twirl on the water, creating a current to bring invertebrates closer to the surface. Shovelers are fairly quiet, but you can hear grunting and quacking from feeding groups.

Huge bill unmistakable. Dark-light-dark-light-dark pattern of male's head and body distinctive even when color can't be seen.

Female's bill like male's but mostly yellow. Body plumage and wings like those of the closely related Blue-winged and Cinnamon Teals.

Cinnamon Teal
Spatula cyanoptera

L 16" | **WS** 22"

Like the Blue-winged Teal, this small, brightly colored duck
is present primarily during summer, with scattered winter
records, and is mostly confined to fresh water. It is fairly
common east, but also breeds sparingly in the Puget Trough,
around Grays Harbor, and along the Lower Columbia River.
Look for it in shallow marshes in the Columbia Basin, where
this is perhaps the commonest dabbling duck after the Mallard.
In the brown plumage worn by females and, in late summer, by
males, this and the Blue-winged are easily confused, making
it difficult to determine their status after the breeding season.
Cinnamon Teals are quiet ducks, sometimes giving soft rattles
and decrescendo calls.

Male a small, bright rusty duck with
red eyes, black bill, and yellow legs.
Powder-blue wing patch and green
speculum, often not visible when
wings closed.

'Female head warmer brown than
Blue-winged, lacking pale throat
and spot behind bill; bill slightly
larger.

Blue-winged Teal

Spatula discors

L 15.5" | **WS** 23"

This little duck is strictly a summer visitor, migrating from as
far south as the tropics to arrive in April. It nests throughout
the eastside and in much smaller numbers west; it is usually
less common than Cinnamon. These ducks breed at shallow
marshy ponds and mostly shun salt water, even in migration,
which is over by September. Varied calls include high-pitched
and low-pitched whistles given by males and single quacks
given by females; decrescendo notes given by both sexes, mostly
on the wintering grounds.

Small dabbling duck with relatively
large bill. Male has shiny gray head
with white face crescent, heavily
black-spotted body with white
flank patch and black behind it.

Female small, with inconspicuous patterning, moderately
large dark bill, pale unstreaked throat, light spot behind bill.
Big pale blue wing patches and iridescent green speculum
usually not visible on water, but distinctive in flight.

American Wigeon

Mareca americana

L 20" | **WS** 32"

American Wigeons are abundant migrants and winterers in the
state, breeding in moderate numbers east and much smaller
numbers west. Along with pintails, they are prominent in
the flocks of thousands of dabbling ducks migrating through
coastal estuaries in early fall, all in dull summer plumage.
Wigeons are the quintessential grazing ducks, with a small
bill adapted for snipping off plant stems and leaves. They can
be common in city parks, grazing on lawns along with Canada
Geese. The call is a high-pitched three-note whistle, like
squeezing a rubber ducky.

Small, mostly blue bill. Male's body plain
reddish-brown, with white flank patch and dark
rear. Head with brilliant green eye stripe and white
crown. Big white forewing patches may be hidden.

Female's plain reddish-brown body
less marked than in other female
dabblers; finely streaked, grayer
head. Bill quite small, mostly blue.

Eurasian Wigeon
Mareca penelope

L 20" | **WS** 32"

Washington is the best place in the Lower 48 to see Eurasian Wigeons. Presumably coming from Siberia, they are widespread in small numbers October–April west, almost always in flocks of American Wigeons; they are much less common east. Between late February and mid-March, 50 or more males have been seen in large flocks of Americans on the Samish Flats west of Edison. Females are distinctly less common, but a few can be found with careful scrutiny. The call is a high-pitched two-note whistle.

Small blue bill and pointed tail; male's body mostly gray, breast salmon, head dark rufous with pale yellowish crown. Notice white-bordered black tertials, white flanks and black rear. White forewing obvious in flight.

Female much like female American Wigeon, but head and neck warm brown, no contrast with body plumage..

Gadwall

Mareca strepera

L 20" | **WS** 33"

Gadwalls are widespread and common throughout the year, but they are never seen in large flocks like most other dabblers. Quite uncommon just a few decades ago, their numbers have increased, first as wintering birds and then as breeding birds, until this is now the second most common breeding duck in western Washington after the Mallard. The increase was brought about at least partly by the increase of invasive Eurasian water milfoil, a favored food in freshwater lakes. Males are mostly silent, while females quack much like female Mallards.

Male mostly gray with black bill and black rear; subtle patterns and colors visible at close range. White speculum often hidden on water but distinctive in flight.

Female much like female Mallard but squarer head, less prominent dark eye line; bill dark along ridge, orange on sides. As in male, white speculum not always visible on resting bird.

Mallard

Anas platyrhynchos

L 23" | **WS** 35"

Mallards are ubiquitous in Washington, primarily on fresh water but also in some numbers in shallow estuaries; they are very common on flooded fields in winter. They nest throughout the state at water bodies of all sizes, from well out in the wilderness to the most urban neighborhoods, as long as there is water where the ducklings can feed on insects and other invertebrates. Mallards nest away from the water's edge, even in a planter box on a houseboat deck. Males call softly *reeb, reeb,* and the repeated loud calls of females are the source of the word *quack*.

Male with brilliant green head, bright yellow bill, white neck ring, and dark chestnut breast contrasting with mostly whitish body. Black uppertail coverts with curled central tail feathers .

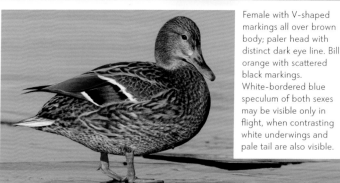

Female with V-shaped markings all over brown body; paler head with distinct dark eye line. Bill orange with scattered black markings. White-bordered blue speculum of both sexes may be visible only in flight, when contrasting white underwings and pale tail are also visible.

Northern Pintail

Anas acuta

L 25" | **WS** 34"

These elegant ducks are abundant in migration and winter throughout the state, gathering food from the bottom of shallow lakes and estuaries with their long neck or wading through flooded fields. Along with Green-winged Teals, they spend much time foraging on tidal flats and roosting in saltmarsh vegetation. Much smaller numbers breed east, only rarely west. Pintails prefer shallow marshy wetlands for nesting, and are thus much affected by droughts, but their numbers remain high across North America. Repeated, low-pitched whistled notes are heard from flocks.

Male with iridescent brown head decorated with white stripe extending from the long white neck. Mostly gray body enhanced by black scapulars, black and white tertials, and very long pin tail.

Speculum partly green in both sexes, bordered buffy in front and white behind. Female's unmarked tan head and long neck contrast with patterned body. Darker bill and shorter tail than male.

Green-winged Teal

Anas crecca

L 14" | **WS** 23"

These small, dark, fast-flying ducks often flock with larger species as they migrate through the state to winter in large numbers in shallow fresh and marine waters. They often feed on intertidal invertebrates, walking across tide flats like plump shorebirds but slurping through the mud like typical dabbling ducks. They are uncommon breeders east, much less common west. The common calls in winter are peeping whistles, higher pitched than those of pintails, with which they often associate.

Male very small; gray with rusty and green head, white vertical side stripe, and black-bordered cream flank patches.

Female very small and heavily patterned. Pale undertail coverts distinctive. Green speculum with white borders may or may not be evident on resting bird, but prominent in flight.

Canvasback

Aythya valisineria

L 21" | **WS** 29"

This large duck with its distinctive profile can be seen on lakes and bays throughout the state in migration, and more locally through the winter, wherever there are aquatic plants with tubers and rhizomes. They also winter near grain elevators on the Snake and Columbia Rivers. Like the other "bay ducks" of the genus *Aythya*, they seem to prefer flocks, sometimes mixing with other species. They are especially conspicuous October–November, even on Lake Washington in Seattle, when mixed flocks of Canvasbacks, Redheads, and scaups pass through the state. They breed in very small numbers in shallow marshy ponds in the east.

Long bill and sloping head profile unique. Male with dark rusty head and neck, red eyes, white body with black at both ends.

Head shape distinctive. Female with sandy to reddish brown and gray body. Gray wing stripes in flight.

Redhead

Aythya americana

L 19" | **WS** 29"

Redheads are fairly common breeders at well-vegetated open lakes and large ponds east, perhaps the most common diving duck breeding in the interior and present from March to mid–September. They are much less common west, quite uncommon breeders and somewhat more common migrants, often seen at sewage ponds. The largest numbers are seen in late fall migration through large parts of the state on lakes and reservoirs, especially east, and smaller numbers remain to winter. Very few are seen on salt water.

Male's head even redder than Canvasback's; blue-gray bill, yellow-orange eyes. Body gray, black at both ends.

Female light brown all over, with faint pale eye ring. Rounded head and dark gray, black-tipped bill. Gray wing stripes in flight.

Lesser Scaup

Aythya affinis

L 16.5" | **WS** 25"

Lesser Scaups are much less common on salt water than Greaters, but occur all along the coast in protected bays. They are present in migration and winter throughout the state, more commonly on fresh water; they are often on smaller water bodies than Greaters. Lessers breed in small numbers on marshy lakes throughout the east and in much smaller numbers west, often at sewage ponds. The two scaups often occur in mixed flocks, permitting close comparison for identification.

Slightly smaller than Greater. White wing stripe shorter, darkens to gray on primaries. Black on bill tip mostly confined to nail. Iridescence on male's more peaked head usually purple.

Female's head peaked. When diving, ducks sleek down their head feathers, making the head shape more difficult to assess.

Greater Scaup

Aythya marila

L 18" | **WS** 28"

Perhaps the most common of the "bay ducks" in Washington, Greater Scaups winter in abundance October–April on protected bays on the outer coast and throughout the Salish Sea. They are common in migration all across the state, and some remain through the winter on larger lakes and reservoirs, with thousands on the Snake and Columbia Rivers. Greater Scaups tend to be in larger flocks than other diving ducks, often associated with scoters.

Male black at both ends and white in the middle. Rounded head, usually with green iridescence. Big blue bill; black on bill tip extends out to either side from nail.

Female all dark brown with conspicuous white face patch. White wing stripe in flight on both secondaries and primaries.

Ring-necked Duck

Aythya collaris

L 17" | **WS** 25"

Ring-necked Ducks are largely restricted to fresh water in Washington, feeding in shallower water than most other diving ducks (those that dive below the surface to feed). They are common in migration throughout the state, and large numbers remain in winter, usually in small flocks scattered over many lakes. This is the only one of the five *Aythya* species to breed on wooded lakes, fairly commonly east and rarely west. None of the species in this genus is particularly vocal.

Male shiny black with gray sides and white blaze on side of breast. Head with prominent peak. Black-tipped gray bill with vivid white ring. Gray wing stripes in flight.

Female has peaked head and ringed bill like the male, but is all brown. Head darker than female Redhead, eye ring more prominent. When present, white patch behind bill less contrasting than in scaup.

Harlequin Duck

Histrionicus histrionicus

L 16.5" | **WS** 26"

Harlequin Ducks are tied to turbulent waters—swift, rocky nesting streams in the Olympics, Cascades, and Northeastern Highlands, and wave-washed, often rocky, shores anywhere along the long coastline during winter. Migrants are rarely seen in the interior. When females begin incubating their eggs, the males migrate to the coast to summer in places such as Dungeness and Protection Island. Because of the turbulence where they usually feed, they leave the water when not foraging and perch on rocks, often in pairs. Interacting groups are noisier, with lots of squeaky whistles, than most of our diving ducks.

Small bill. Often perches out of the water on rocks. Male strikingly blue-gray, black, white, and reddish.

Female all dark brown; head patterning much like female scoter, but with much smaller bill.

Surf Scoter
Melanitta perspicillata

L 20" | **WS** 30"

Surf Scoters are abundant and widespread winterers in
all coastal waters; they are often associated with rocky
shores, where they find the mussels that are such an important
part of their diet. They commonly feed from mussel-covered
pilings in protected waters but can also be found riding
the big waves of the outer coast, diving for bivalves and
other invertebrates. They are very common migrants off
the outer beaches in May and September. Small groups of
immatures may be found locally in summer. They are also
rare migrants September–November on large lakes in the
interior. The male's wings whistle in flight, including during
spectacular courtship displays.

Male black with big, brightly colored bill
and white head patches fore and aft,
enhanced further by white eyes. First-year
males have smaller or no head patches.

Female all brown with
unfeathered bill base, three
white head patches. White
nape patch absent in juveniles.

White-winged Scoter

Melanitta deglandi

L 21" **WS** 34"

The largest of our ducks, this species is more often found on large bays than the other scoters, as it feeds primarily on clams that inhabit sandy substrates. Like Surf Scoters, White-wings migrate in large numbers along the outer coast in spring and fall, sometimes well out at sea. They are also rare fall migrants in the interior. Immatures remain through the summer at scattered coastal locations. Wintering birds are usually silent, and the wings of males do not whistle in flight as in the other scoters.

Male slightly larger than Surf Scoter. Bright-billed, but with white only around eyes. White wing patches often hidden, but dazzling when visible.

Female resembles Surf Scoter if white wing patches can't be seen. Mature female with all brown head, immatures with white spots somewhat like Surf. Note feathered bill base.

Black Scoter

Melanitta americana

L 19" | **WS** 28"

By far the least common of the scoters, Black Scoters occur widely along the coast but usually in very small numbers, and they are very rare fall migrants in the interior. They are more likely found along rocky shores with Surf Scoters than in sandy bays with White-winged. All three scoters, sometimes in large concentrations, feed on herring spawn in spring. Males' wings whistle in flight, and courting males continuously utter a loud, mournful *whoooooo*.

Male black with a "blob of butter" on the bill base. Head rounder and shorter than in other scoters. Primaries paler than rest of wing in flight.

Female's head shape and pale cheeks and throat distinctive. Similarly patterned Ruddy Duck is much smaller.

Long-tailed Duck

Clangula hyemalis

L 21" | **WS** 28"

Long-tailed Ducks are winter visitors in small flocks all along the coast, distinctly more common in the northern half of the Salish Sea. Point Roberts and Blaine/Semiahmoo Spit are good locations. Most are seen well offshore, as they feed in deeper water than other sea ducks. They are rare in the interior, found mostly in late fall on reservoirs along the Columbia River. The males give wonderful loud *out-outaluck* or *owl-omelette* calls.

Elegant, mostly pale duck with dark cheek patch. Male has long tail a pintail would envy. Small, pink-banded bill. Molts into darker plumage in spring, brown above with black head and neck, white cheeks.

Female has dark back, mostly white head with dark cheek patch. More brown on head in spring. In both sexes, all-dark wings in flight.

Common Goldeneye

Bucephala clangula

L 18.5" | **WS** 26"

Common migrants throughout the state, Common Goldeneyes
also winter along the coast and on rivers and ice-free lakes,
usually in smaller groups than Barrow's. With other ducks, they
are numerous at grain facilities on the Snake and Columbia
Rivers. They dive frequently for clams, crabs, and other marine
invertebrates. Watch for late winter and spring courtship
behavior, spectacular in both goldeneyes and Bufflehead.
Flying goldeneyes look short-necked, and males' wings whistle
rhythmically in flight. As in other ducks, the distinctive head
shape may be obscured by flattening the feathers when they are
actively diving. Displaying males give a soft *peent* call.

Male with bright yellow eyes and
white circle on peaked black head
(green in sun); white breast and sides.
Big white wing patches in flight.

Female's rich dark brown head
contrasts with duller
gray-brown body. Black bill
usually with yellow tip. Smaller
white wing patches than male.

Barrow's Goldeneye

Bucephala islandica

L 18" | **WS** 28"

Barrow's Goldeneyes occur throughout the Salish Sea in winter, especially where there are concentrations of mussels at such sites as Penn Cove, Hood Canal, and the pilings at ferry landings. They are almost always seen in small flocks, often with Surf Scoters. Migrants are locally common on freshwater lakes and rivers, many of them remaining through the winter. They are fairly common breeders at mountain lakes all across the state. Wings of males whistle rhythmically in flight, and males give a soft, two-note grunting call in courtship display.

Male with bright yellow eyes and white crescent on puffy black head (mostly purple in sun); white breast and sides, black point at side of breast. Big white wing patches in flight.

Female's head puffier than in Common; bill smaller, yellow-orange in winter. Smaller white wing patches than male. In females and immatures, head shape is best distinction from Common Goldeneye.

Bufflehead

Bucephala albeola

L 13.5" | **WS** 21"

Buffleheads are some of our most ubiquitous ducks, widespread migrants and winterers on both fresh and salt water. They are more common in protected waters of the Salish Sea than on the open sea, and they are likely to be on smaller water bodies than other diving ducks, even little ponds. While some other seagoing ducks have declined recently, Bufflehead population have been stable. There are scattered breeding records from wooded lakes in the northeast part of the state, including Big Meadows and Bonaparte Lakes.

Male is a tiny diver with all white sides, big white patch on puffy head. Head looks black and white in cloudy weather, iridescent in sunlight. Big white wing patches in flight.

Female mostly brown, with distinctive white slash on dark head. Smaller white wing patches than male.

Hooded Merganser

Lophodytes cucullatus

L 18" | **WS** 24"

Hooded Mergansers breed in small numbers at wooded lakes throughout the state, but are more widespread during migration. They winter widely on fresh water, more common west, and are found on small ponds, lakes, and rivers. Smaller numbers winter on salt water throughout the Salish Sea, usually in pairs. They have increased in recent years, perhaps because they freely use nest boxes provided for Wood Ducks.

Male strikingly patterned with narrow bill. Puffy, mostly white crest may be folded to a narrow white bar; much more white shows when expanded. Reddish sides distinguish from male Bufflehead. Gray patch on coverts, white secondaries in flight.

Female brown with white-streaked tertials and puffy crest that may be folded. Slender bill partly yellow. Small white wing patch in flight.

Common Merganser

Mergus merganser

L 25" | **WS** 34"

Common Mergansers breed widely across the state on larger lowland and mid-elevation rivers; adults and young move down to the river mouths in midsummer. Many more arrive from the north in autumn to winter on lakes and in marine channels with clear water and swift currents, for example, among the San Juan Islands. Many hundreds are sometimes seen east soon after lakes open in late winter. Large numbers can be seen feeding where schooling fish are abundant. They often submerge their heads while swimming, looking for fish.

Large duck with slender, red bill. Male very white with black head and back. Big white wing patches in flight.

Female plain gray with contrasting rich brown head and white throat, narrow red bill. Shaggy crest. Smaller white wing patches than male.

Red-breasted Merganser

Mergus serrator

L 23" | **WS** 30"

Red-breasted Mergansers are winter visitors from their arctic and subarctic breeding grounds. Individuals and small flocks are common in most marine habitats from October to early May. Much smaller numbers occur on lakes and rivers all over the state in migration and winter. At times in spring, very large flocks dive synchronously to capture herrings spawning in shallow bays. Watch for the spectacular courtship display of males in late winter and spring.

Smaller than Common Merganser. Male with reddish bill, red eyes, ragged crest, and complex pattern including reddish breast. Big white wing patches in flight

Female shows little contrast between reddish head and brown body; orange bill. Crest ragged. Smaller white wing patches than male.

Ruddy Duck

Oxyura jamaicensis

L 15" | **WS** 23"

Ruddy Ducks look like the ideal bathtub ducks. They are fairly common breeders on marshy lakes and ponds east of the Cascades, occasionally on sewage lagoons west. They winter on freshwater lakes and shallow bays, often in large flocks. With prey abundant in the bottom mud, they fill themselves up in feeding bouts and then nap for hours. Males wear their breeding plumage in summer rather than in winter like other ducks, perform their courtship behavior only on the breeding grounds, and contribute to parental care. In his courtship display, the male makes a "motorboat" sound by smacking his bill on his chest, then runs along the water.

Breeding male with spectacular sky-blue bill, white cheeks, and ruddy body. Long tail often cocked, especially in courtship display.

Nonbreeding male brown, but identified by broad bill, white cheeks, and long tilted tail.

Female has muted colors with dark crown and cheek stripe, characteristic tail.

Mountain Quail

Oreortyx pictus

L 11" | **WS** 16"

Mountain Quails are uncommon and local residents, known only from oak stands in Klickitat County and low areas along Snake River tributaries in the Blue Mountains foothills; an introduced population is found in second-growth woodland in south Puget Sound in Mason and Kitsap Counties. They are probably declining in all three regions. They are secretive, usually in dense cover and difficult to see, and most likely to be found by the calls of the males in spring, a loud, clear, two-note whistled *quee-ark*. Winter flock members give sharp, whistled calls to stay in contact.

The harlequin of the uplands: beautiful rusty, brown, and gray body vividly marked with white. Head adorned with two black plumes.

California Quail

Callipepla californica

L 10" | **WS** 14"

This introduced species is a common resident of urban and farmland habitats in eastern Washington and locally so in the west, wherever there is a combination of open ground for feeding and dense brush for retreating. Urbanization and rats have greatly reduced their numbers west. Flocks of up to a few dozen birds form in winter, keeping together with an almost constant staccato *pit-pit-pit-pit*. The male's spring *chi-CA-go* call is unmistakable.

Male (below) gray with streaked sides, scaly belly, brightly patterned head, and black topknot of six feathers. Female (left) lacks striking head colors; topknot much smaller.

Chukar
Alectoris chukar

L 14" **WS** 20"

This non-native partridge, introduced to the state from Eurasia in 1931, is a rock-dweller. Look for Chukars anywhere there are canyons or rocky hillsides above rivers in the Columbia Basin, around the Blue Mountains, and up the Okanogan River. They prefer open habitat with sagebrush and grasses, especially the introduced cheat grass, their favorite winter food. Pairs and small, occasionally large, flocks are seen through the winter. Watch for males calling from the tops of rimrock in spring. The guttural rolling call, which includes sounds something like "chukar," resounds from the hillsides as they pair off.

Vividly marked desert partridge. White throat outlined in black, barred flanks, red bill and legs. Rusty-tipped tail in flight.

Gray Partridge
Perdix perdix

L 12.5" | **WS** 19"

Native to Europe, Gray Partridges were introduced for hunting around 1900 and became common residents in open and lightly wooded grasslands in and around the Columbia Basin. They are still locally common, more so in the open sagebrush and wheat-fields on the edges of the basin than in the denser sagebrush of the dry central basin ; they are declining over much of their range as their habitat is lost to modern agriculture. The Yakima Training Center and other parts of Yakima and eastern Kittitas Counties are good places to look, as well as the Waterville Plateau and Palouse country south of Spokane. Males give a "rusty gate" call in spring, and members of a flock give *kuta-kut-kut-kut* alarm calls.

Gray-brown, finely barred, with white-streaked and rusty-barred sides. Large rusty belly patch not always visible, but rusty tail prominent in flight.

Ring-necked Pheasant

Phasianus colchicus

L 35" | **WS** 31"

Ring-necked Pheasants are long-time residents of Washington. Native to Asia, they were first introduced for hunting in the late 1800s, and they continue to be released. They are common in many areas east, as they thrive in farmlands, including wheatfields, as well as native grassland. Look for them in areas with shrub cover and at the edges of riparian woodland. They are much more local and declining in the Puget Sound lowlands of western Washington. In spring, males give a loud, double-note staccato crow, accented on the second syllable, often followed by noisy wing flaps.

Male a long-tailed, beautifully plumaged "chicken" with iridescent dark head, bare red face, and wide white neck ring.

Female pale like open-country grouse, but with very long tail. Flight steady, with no rocking.

Greater Sage-Grouse

Centrocercus urophasianus

L 28" | **WS** 38"

Sage-grouse survive in remnant populations totaling just hundreds in the Columbia Basin, and the species continues to decline as shrub steppe is lost to cropland; it is now listed as Threatened in Washington. One population is in Moses Coulee and rougher parts of the Waterville Plateau, another on the Yakima Training Center, and a smaller number are found on Crab Creek, with a total of 21 display grounds, or leks. Populations are kept stable only by translocating grouse from other states. Small flocks wander well away from lekking sites, even to the edge of agriculture, but they must have sagebrush for their winter food. Numerous males come together in spring to compete vigorously for females attracted to the lek; displaying males make musical bubbling sounds.

Longish tail, large black belly patch, male with mostly white breast. Flies with rocking motion. Male's spectacular display with spread tail, white-tipped undertail coverts, inflated breast sacs.

Ruffed Grouse

Bonasa umbellus

L 17" | **WS** 22"

This grouse is resident throughout Washington wherever there
are stands of deciduous trees, including riparian woodland and
mixed broadleaf and conifer forest. East of the Cascades, this
includes the Blue Mountains and the Northeastern Highlands,
where birds vary from quite gray to more reddish. Birds on
the Olympic Peninsula are especially dark reddish, matching
the colors of the deep woodlands. Woodland-dwelling grouse
are difficult birds to see, most often seen at the roadside when
females are shepherding their broods in late summer. There
are more insects in such open areas for the young to eat. This
species is largely silent, but the male's deep drumming can be
heard in spring.

"Chicken" with tufted
head, richly marked body
and black neck patch. Tail
rusty (mostly coastal) or
gray (mostly interior), with
broad black bar at tip.

Spruce Grouse

Falcipennis canadensis

L 16" | **WS** 22"

These compact grouse occur at elevations above 4,000 feet on the east side of the Cascades south to Yakima County and in the Northeastern Highlands. They are fairly common, but quite hard to see in stands of lodgepole pine and Engelmann spruce. To see them, drive through these habitats in late summer when females are caring for chicks. They may move locally between optimal winter and summer foraging sites. The summer diet includes leaves, flowers, blueberries, and even some insects, but they rely on spruce and pine needles in winter. Displaying males in spring give deep hoots.

Female smaller than Dusky Grouse. Speckled and barred rich brown and white, with white-tipped uppertail coverts.

Male a very dark upland forest grouse, breast and throat black, back barred, sides spotted. Tail black with white-tipped uppertail coverts.

White-tailed Ptarmigan

Lagopus leucurus

L 12.5" | **WS** 22"

Ptarmigans are found only in the alpine zone of the Cascades, south to Mount Adams. These birds are amazingly well camouflaged and tend not to flush, but they are nevertheless regularly seen above Artist's Point on Mount Baker and above Paradise and Sunrise on Mount Rainier; they are also present along many other high-altitude hiking trails. Easternmost records are at Slate Peak, where birds in completely white plumage have been seen from the road in autumn, and at Chopaka Mountain. Some move to nonbreeding areas in winter, even down to the edge of conifer forest, and skiers sometimes see small flocks. Best chances to see them are in late summer, when females have chicks. Male song is a weird combination of chucks, chatters, and screams.

Alpine grouse. Breeding male white with black markings; red comb.

Breeding female mottled brown all over. White tail evident in flight.

Nonbreeding plumage as white as a bird can be, with black eyes and bill, fully feathered feet.

Sooty Grouse

Dendragapus fuliginosus

L 20" | **WS** 26"

Sooty Grouse are widely resident on the westside well up in altitude in the Cascades and Olympics, but are scarce in the Puget Sound lowlands. Subalpine meadows at Mount Rainier and Hurricane Ridge are good sites in summer. Males display from trees in spring, giving a series low-pitched hoots and showing a "fried egg" on each side of the neck as white-based feathers open to show bare yellow skin. Later in the season, look for females with broods in mountain meadows. The young stay with the female until fully grown.

Large forest and subalpine grouse; dark tail with fairly wide gray tip. Male (below) with mottled upperparts, gray head, neck, and underparts. Bare skin of displaying male yellow. Female (left) much more mottled brown and smaller than male. Tail pattern best distinction from other forest grouse.

Dusky Grouse

Dendragapus obscurus

L 20" | **WS** 26"

The Sooty and the Dusky Grouse replace each other in Washington's conifer forests. Duskies occur on the east side of the North Cascades and in all the wooded mountain ranges to the east. They are often seen on the roadside in Okanogan County, where in fall and winter they undertake lengthy migrations on foot from the lower slopes up into the high country. Male Dusky Grouse display on the ground, with hoots similar to those of Sooty, but the fried egg on the side of their neck has a red yolk.

Much like Sooty; the two species overlap slightly in North Cascades to Okanogan River. Tail in both sexes without gray tip. Bare neck sacs of displaying male red.

Sharp-tailed Grouse
Tympanuchus phasianellus

L 17" | **WS** 26"

Vanishing from Washington as native grasslands disappear, Sharp-tailed Grouse are listed as endangered in the state. They are now limited to a few scattered populations in Okanogan, Douglas, and Lincoln Counties. Leks are monitored by wildlife biologists, and their location is not publicized. Viewing this grouse is easiest in winter, when small flocks feed on birch and aspen buds in river valleys in the Omak/Okanogan area, for example, Scotch Creek, Chesaw, and Swanson Lakes WAs. Displaying male rattles feathers and gurgles. Flushed birds give loud *tuk-tuk-tuk* or *tucker-tucker-tucker* calls and rock from side to side in flight.

Heavily mottled prairie grouse, pointed tail with buffy to white outer feathers. Displaying male with yellow combs and purple neck skin.

Female like male but no colored skin, central tail feathers more heavily barred.

Wild Turkey

Meleagris gallopavo

L 46" | **WS** 64"

Wild Turkeys were unsuccesfully brought to Washington beginning a century ago, but more recent introductions created populations that have flourished and spread. Turkeys are now widespread in forested areas all around the Columbia Basin and in river valleys in the northeast; they seem to thrive most in oak and ponderosa pine woodland. Large winter flocks have been seen along the road east of Loomis. There is also a long-established but local population on San Juan Island. For a bird that is hunted, turkeys are surprisingly tame in many areas. Males give their well-known gobbles in spring, and all males in earshot will respond with their own in a cacophony.

Male is the unmistakable Thanksgiving bird, becoming more common and widespread in the state.

Female smaller than male, with blue-gray naked skin, no "beard" on breast, and no display.

Eared Grebe

Podiceps nigricollis

L 13" | **WS** 16"

Eared Grebes are very local breeders on marshy lakes and ponds in the northern part of the Columbia Basin. Turnbull NWR and Lake Lenore have colonies. A few birds remain on eastside lakes through the winter, including Soap Lake, where they are common in migration. They are quite uncommon in migration and winter west, but small numbers occur in bays, such as Birch Bay and inside Ediz Hook. Many swimming invertebrates are taken by these petite grebes, and they find good feeding opportunities on sewage ponds and the highly productive Grand Coulee lakes. On the breeding grounds, they give rising, squealed *poo-EE-chk* calls

Small grebe with petite, slightly upturned bill and fiery red eyes. Breeding birds have golden "ears" on black neck.

Nonbreeding birds distinguished from Horned by mostly brown neck and puffy crest. Often rides higher in water, with a high stern.

Horned Grebe

Podiceps auritus

L 14" | **WS** 18"

Horned Grebes are common winterers September to early May throughout the Salish Sea and on larger lakes and reservoirs, often in small flocks and occasionally in groups of 100 or more. A few pairs breed at marshy lakes in the northeast corner of the state, including Turnbull NWR. They feed on shrimp and on bottom fish such as sculpins and gunnels. They sometimes dive with scoters to take advantage of the prey the larger birds flush underwater. Like other wintering grebes, they molt into full breeding plumage before leaving the wintering area. On breeding grounds, they give wavering and squealing calls, sometimes ending in a rattle.

Breeding birds with straight, slender dark bill, golden "horns" on black head, brilliant red eyes, and rufous neck and sides.

Nonbreeding birds with black cap and extensive white cheeks, chin, and foreneck. Bill becomes pale.

Red-necked Grebe

Podiceps grisegena

L 18" | **WS** 24"

Red-necked Grebes are common September–April in the Salish
Sea, less so in outer coastal bays, often feeding in kelp beds.
Eel-like gunnels are a favorite prey, taken from the bottom;
watch diving grebes to see one of these marine fish brought to
the surface and mandibulated. Smaller numbers also winter
on large lakes and reservoirs elsewhere in the state, especially
along the Columbia River. Breeding birds, often in small colonies, are scattered on marshy lakes from Okanogan County east.
Molson Lake and lakes in the Sinlahekin WA have had them
in recent years. Very vocal on breeding grounds, with honks
and whinnies.

Large grebe, in breeding
plumage with black crown, white
cheeks, and rusty neck. Large
bill mostly blackish. Eyes brown,
unlike other marine grebes.

Nonbreeding birds very plain
brown, with whitish throat and
mostly yellow bill. Somewhat
loonlike in appearance.

Pied-billed Grebe

Podilymbus podiceps

L 13" | **WS** 16"

This is the most ubiquitous grebe in the state, breeding at
nearly all lakes and ponds with some emergent vegetation. In
winter, many move to larger bodies of water, including reservoirs on the Snake and Columbia River and even the salt water
of the Salish Sea. Like other grebes, they migrate at night, and
only rarely fly in daytime. The floating nests are easy to spot,
and the whole cycle can be watched at urban lakes and ponds
such as Magnuson Park and Green Lake in Seattle. Stripe-
headed young chicks are carried on their parent's back. Both
sexes give a long series of *kuk kuk kuk* and *cow cow cow cow*
territorial calls.

Small grebe; like
other grebes,
virtually tailless.
Breeding birds
with black-banded
chicken-like bill
and black throat.

Nonbreeding
birds with
plain head
and bill.

Western Grebe

Aechmophorus occidentalis

L 25" | **WS** 24"

Swan-necked Western Grebes arrive in May to breed in colonies on some larger lakes in the Columbia Basin, for example Moses and Banks Lakes and the Potholes Reservoir. Watch for their spectacular courtship display early in the breeding season. They migrate in September to large lakes, reservoirs, and coastal bays, where they winter in flocks well offshore, feeding on schooling surface fish such as herring and sand lance. Formerly abundant in winter, they have become much less common; many have shifted their winter range south to California. Calls on breeding grounds are high-pitched and creaky.

Large, formally patterned grebe with long, swanlike black and white neck; crown black around eyes. Bill dull yellowish, dark above and below.

Clark's Grebe

Aechmophorus clarkii

L 25" | **WS** 24"

Clark's Grebes breed at the same lakes as Westerns, although in smaller numbers, and they can often be seen together. Clark's is distinguished by paler sides and more extensive white on the head and neck. Both build floating nests out in the open, and both carry their young on their back, then lead them around and catch fish for them until they fledge. Downy young of Clark's are paler than those of Westerns. The two species are identical in habits, but the creaky call of Clark's is single, that of Western doubled. Almost all Clark's leave the state to winter in California.

Like Western Grebe but sides paler, black of crown ends above eye. Bill brighter orange-yellow.

Rock Pigeon

Columba livia

L 12.5" | **WS** 28"

This familiar but highly variable bird, introduced throughout North America long ago, is now found wherever there are human populations, from deep in the largest cities to farmlands throughout the state, nesting on buildings and bridges. Watch for small flocks evenly perched along power lines running along streets and highways; they nest under nearby overpasses. But they also occur well away from people, nesting on ledges such as those in the Columbia River gorge and Yakima Canyon, and commuting to farmland some distance away to feed on grain. Flocks fly with loud wing clapping. Males give a rolling *coo*, usually during intense courtship display.

Familiar city pigeon, strutting on lawns and streets. Wild type bluish gray with black markings on wings and tail, but feral birds vary in color from white to black. Most with dark terminal tail band; wing linings contrastingly white in all but darkest birds.

Band-tailed Pigeon

Patagioenas fasciata

L 14.5" | **WS** 26"

Band-tailed Pigeons are resident west, but many migrate south, leaving smaller numbers to winter. They are also seen occasionally east, where there are no substantial populations. They occur in all wooded habitats, including urban and suburban parks and neighborhoods, and nest high in trees. They are the largest birds that regularly visit feeders, where they can be appreciated at close range as a flock cleans out a full feeder in half an hour. Males give a loud, double owl-like hoot from a treetop, often before and after display flights with shallow wingbeats above the trees.

Big gray and mauve forest pigeon with yellow bill and feet, white neck collar. Tail with narrow dark subterminal band and paler tip. Juveniles duller, without collar.

Eurasian Collared-Dove
Streptopelia decaocto

L 13" | **WS** 22"

These non-native doves, first seen in Washington in 2000, have become common and widespread residents throughout the state. They are country birds, most often seen in small towns and farmland where there are abundant supplies of grain, but are absent from heavily wooded areas and inner cities. They are ubiquitous in the open country east of the Cascades but much more local west, for example, at Dungeness and Edison. They are often seen on wires or displaying overhead with shallow wingbeats. They also come to bird feeders in some places. Males give a characteristic three-note coo, the middle note higher and longer: *ex-HAUS-ted.*

Large dove of the countryside, larger and paler than Mourning. Broad square tail with extensive white tip. Narrow black neck collar, lacking in juvenile.

Mourning Dove

Zenaida macroura

L 12" **WS** 18"

Mourning Doves occur statewide, but are much more common east, where semi-open country provides them with tall shrubs and scattered trees in which to nest and open, weed-filled fields furnish seeds. In western Washington they are as local as collared-doves, occurring in the same open areas with scattered tree groves. They are migratory on both sides, with much greater numbers in summer and small flocks concentrated at few sites in winter. Collared-doves may be displacing this native species on the eastside. The male Mourning Dove has a distinctive *coo-a-coo-coo-coo* call, and the wings of both sexes whistle in flight.

Plain brown dove of the countryside, with red feet, black spots on wings, and long, pointed tail with white-tipped outer feathers. Male usually with blue-gray crown. Juvenile heavily scalloped above.

Common Nighthawk

Chordeiles minor

L 9.5" | **WS** 24"

Nighthawks are migrants from far away, appearing in late May and mostly gone by the end of August. They have largely disappeared from western Washington, where they formerly inhabited cities and countryside alike. They are still common east, although declining there also. They nest on the ground but roost in trees, sometimes gathering in wooded groves before departing for the wintering areas in South America. The loud *peent* call is characteristic, as is the *vrooom* made by the male's wings at the end of his diving display flight.

Long, pointed wings with prominent white band across primaries. White tail band in male. Erratic flight, ranging from just above the ground to high in the air, usually at dusk.

Camouflaged upperparts, barred underparts, tiny bill, large eyes, and long pointed wings. White band across throat prominent in male, reduced in female. Usually perches parallel to the branch rather than across it.

Common Poorwill

Phalaenoptilus nuttallii

L 8" | **WS** 17"

Poorwills inhabit the transition zone between ponderosa pine and shrub steppe east of the Cascades, usually in habitats with good shrub growth and open woodland. Present April–September, they are very difficult to see during the day, but they start to feed just after dusk, and can be seen at night by slowly driving on gravel roads. They are often found by their orange eye shine, reflecting headlights or a flashlight. Any of the canyon roads is a good bet, for example, Robinson and Manastash Canyons. Call is a loud, repeated *poor-WILL*, sometimes with a barely audible third note.

Compact, ground-roosting nightjar, rarely visible until it comes out into the open in the evening. Tiny bill but big mouth; large eyes. Perhaps the best camouflaged of any of our birds.

Black Swift

Cypseloides niger

L 7" | **WS** 18"

Superb flying machines, Black Swifts are mystery birds in
Washington. Present May–September, they nest behind water-
falls or in other inaccessible places at scattered locations from
the coast (Cape Flattery) to both sides of the Cascades; they
may nest near Copper Mountain, Newhalem, and Stehekin.
Long-distance fliers, they are often seen far from nest sites.
During stormy weather in the Cascades, flocks descend to
the western lowlands to hunt for flying insects, for example,
foraging low over Lake Washington in August. Around the nest
they give sharp, twittering chips, often in a very rapid series.

Long-winged, often high-flying
all-black swift with notched
tail. Never seen perched
except at mostly inaccessible
nest sites. Females with
extensive white tips to feathers
of underparts, not easy to see.

Vaux's Swift

Chaetura vauxi

L 5" | **WS** 12"

This small swift is a summer visitor May–September, occurring throughout the west and in all forested regions east, even in suburbs. Originally nesting in hollow snags in old-growth forests, their numbers have declined historically with the decline of those forests. They also nest in secondary forests with suitable nest sites, and they have adapted to human presence by switching to chimneys in some areas, although not in the open Columbia Basin. Thousands may roost Aug–Sep in large urban chimneys while staging for fall migration, for example, at Monroe, Olympia, and Yakima. Calls are very high-pitched, rapid chipping or twittering.

Small gray-brown swift with paler throat, stubby tail, very rapid "twinkling" wingbeat. Best seen at chimneys used for fall roosts.

White-throated Swift

Aeronautes saxatilis

L 6.5" | **WS** 15"

Present from late March through September, White-throated Swifts are birds of dry canyons in and around the Columbia Basin, nesting above all the major rivers and coulee lakes. They are true birds of the air, even copulating in flight. They build their nests in cliff crevices and fly out over the countryside to forage for insects, often so high in the air as to be nearly invisible. Stand on the rim of one of the cliffs, such as Frenchman Coulee or Dry Falls in the Lower Grand Coulee, and you may be thrilled by birds flying right past your eyes at what seem like supersonic speeds. They make a continuous loud, high-pitched twittering as they pass.

Dark brown and white swift of dry canyons. White secondary tips and flank patches visible from above. Much longer wings and faster, straighter flight than Violet-green Swallow.

Black-chinned Hummingbird

Archilochus alexandri

L 4" | **WS** 5"

Look for Black-chinned Hummingbirds from May to mid-August in lower-elevation riparian woodland and deciduous groves from Yakima County north along the lower east slope of the Cascades and in the forested regions east of the Columbia Basin. They take nectar at shrub and herb flowers in clearings, and are attracted to feeders anywhere, even in the suburbs. They have increased in recent years, probably from the profusion of feeders. The calls are a great variety of chip notes.

Male dull green above, whitish below with greenish-tinged gray sides. Black throat bordered below by not always visible violet band. Tail shallowly forked; outer feathers pointed, with pale tips.

Female (right) dull green above, mostly white below. Tail with white corners. Bill slightly longer than in other local hummingbirds, a good mark for both sexes.

Anna's Hummingbird

Calypte anna

L 4" | **WS** 5"

This hummingbird of suburban gardens is an example of a species adapting to the presence of humans and expanding its range dramatically. Not seen in Washington until 1964, it began nesting by 1976, and continues to increase in the lowlands of western Washington, where it is resident everywhere, especially in suburban settings. This is our only winter hummer, presumably subsidized year-round by hummingbird feeders. It has spread slowly across the Cascades and is now fairly common in Wenatchee, Ellensburg, and Yakima, but records are still scattered east of the Columbia River, where there may be no permanent populations yet. Males have a more complex song than other hummers; in their flight display, they ascend high into the air and plummet down, making an explosive squeak at the bottom of the dive as the air passes through their outer tail feathers.

Male (left) brilliant green above, gray below with green scallops on sides. Crown and wide gorget brilliant red or blackish, depending on light. All-dark tail shallowly forked. Female (bottom) larger and grayer below than Black-chinned. Sometimes a few red feathers on throat; immature males show more red. Tail rounded, outer feathers tipped white.

Rufous Hummingbird

Selasphorus rufus

L 4" | **WS** 4.5"

Rufous are the most common hummingbirds in Washington, breeding statewide in areas of open woodland. One of the earliest migrants, they arrive as early as late February. They are easily seen at feeders, sometimes in large numbers, and it is entertaining as well as educational to watch their aggressive interactions. Early breeders, they migrate—males first, followed by the females and young— up to mountain meadows, where red wildflowers feed them as they prepare for the southward journey to Mexico; all are gone by mid-September. Hummers chip constantly at each other. Males' wings whine in flight. The spectacular display flight, directed at a perched female, takes the male through the air in a vertical oval, at the bottom of which the narrow outer primaries create a brief but surprisingly loud staccato burst.

Male (above) rich reddish all over, with white breast. Gorget fiery red in the right light. Only hummer with pointed tail; all tail feathers pointed, reddish with brown tips. Female (right) green above with reddish-tinged rump and mostly reddish tail feathers. Tail dark-tipped and white-cornered. White below, with dark streaks on throat and rusty sides.

Calliope Hummingbird

Selasphorus calliope

L 3" | **WS** 4"

Calliope Hummingbirds are common summer residents from late April to early September in open forests on the east side of the Cascades, in the Northeastern Highlands, and in the Blue Mountains. Ponderosa pine, grand fir, and Douglas-fir are common trees in their preferred habitat, which must also include clearings and tall shrubs where the males sing and display and where nests are placed. They are attracted to hummingbird feeders, where they twitter like other hummers as they interact. The male's display dive ends with a metallic *pzzt-zing* at the bottom.

Our smallest hummingbird, quite short-billed. Male green above, white to pale gray below. Rays of red-violet feathers form a lovely broad gorget (throat feathers). Forked black tail.

Female much like Rufous but smaller, shorter-billed, and shorter-tailed. A bit paler on sides, very little reddish in tail. Hovering birds often hold body horizontal.

American Coot

Fulica americana

L 15.5" | **WS** 24"

Coots are common breeders in marshy lakes in the Puget Sound lowlands and almost ubiquitous in the lowlands east of the Cascades. They are absent only from the outer parts of the Olympic Peninsula and high-elevation lakes. Watch for adults feeding their brightly colored chicks. Tens of thousands have been estimated at Columbia and Turnbull NWRs in migration, and Lake Washington hosts large flocks. In winter, huge flocks sometimes gather on larger lakes and rivers, and many move into protected coastal bays and estuaries. Basically vegetarians, coots often leave their wetland habitat to graze on urban lawns, where their big feet with lobed toes are visible. They have many grunting, croaking, and squawking notes, vaguely chicken-like.

This member of the rail family swims and occasionally dives. Easily distinguished from ducks by dark gray body with darker head and neck, bright red eye, chicken-like white bill. Juvenile gray-brown with whitish head and neck, darker bill.

Sora
Porzana carolina

L 9" | **WS** 14"

Soras occur widely in the state except for the west side of the Olympic Peninsula and around the Blue Mountains. They are common only April–October, and are absent or rare in winter. They are more common than the Virginia Rail east of the Cascades, where they breed in more open sedge and grass marshes or wet meadows; they also occur at higher elevations than the Virginia. Confused migrants have been found on city streets on rainy nights and high on ridges in the shrub steppe. Both species eat aquatic plants and animals. Both male and female Soras give a loud *tereee* call repeated at intervals, often ending with a long whinny; the whinny call is also commonly given without the introduction.

Sedge-marsh skulker with short, bright yellow bill and black face patch. Richly patterned brown back, gray underparts with barred sides. Undertail coverts mostly white. Immature shades of brown all over with no face patch, short brown and orange bill.

Virginia Rail
Rallus limicola

L 9.5" | **WS** 13"

Virginia Rails inhabit extensive dense cattail and bulrush marshes throughout the state, from the lowlands to middle elevations. The strident *kik-kik-kik-kik-kadik-kadik-kadik* of the male is a sure sign of their presence; pairs duet with grunting *unh unh unh unh unh* calls, like pigs in the marsh. Common April–October; many leave the state in winter, particularly east, and those that remain are quiet, making them much more difficult to detect. Though marshes have been destroyed by human settlement and agriculture, Virginia Rail populations may have increased in recent decades as heavy winter freezes have become less frequent, making it easier for the birds to find food.

Long-billed, skulking cattail-marsh bird, mostly rusty, with gray cheeks. Mottled above and barred on sides. Tail often cocked, with patterned undertail coverts. Juvenile mottled blackish below.

Sandhill Crane

Antigone canadensis

L 47" | **WS** 79"

Sandhill Cranes from the Arctic migrate through Washington by the thousands March–April and September–October, often soaring high in the sky. They appear widely in the Columbia Basin, including along Lower Crab Creek in spring and the Grand Coulee in fall. A large flight also passes Cape Flattery in April and May. The only wintering birds are in the Lower Columbia River bottomlands, primarily in Clark County. There is a small breeding population at Conboy Lake and in the uplands of the Yakama Indian Reservation, arriving in March and leaving in October. Cranes have a varied diet, from seeds and worms to nestling birds, but in many areas they have shifted to cultivated grains. Calls are an unmistakable bugling.

Large, long-legged, sharp-billed waterbird, foraging more on land than in water. Shape quite distinct from Great Blue Heron, with big "bustle" over wing tip and tail. Gray all over, tinged with brown; red crown with hairlike feathers.

In flight, neck always extended, in contrast with Great Blue Heron. Flies with upward flick of wings on each beat.

Black Oystercatcher

Haematopus bachmani

L 17.5" | **WS** 32"

The loud *wheeep wheeep wheeep* calls advertise the presence of oystercatchers, as if the voice were necessary to call attention to this striking bird, mistakable for nothing else but perhaps a crow carrying a firecracker. Oystercatchers breed on rocky shores on the outer coast south to Point Grenville, with perhaps a few at Cape Disappointment; they also breed everywhere on the Salish Sea south to Admiralty Inlet. Pairs are often seen together, edging limpets off rocks and deftly de-shelling them before a quick swallow. Boating around the San Juan Islands is a good way to see them, and large numbers roost in winter on rocks at West Beach in Deception Pass State Park.

Big, noisy, rock-foraging shorebird; brown tinge of back visible at close range. Unmistakable, with chisel-shaped red-orange bill and short pinkish legs. Female has tiny black spot in bright yellow eye, usually absent in male. Juvenile with dark bill tip.

American Avocet

Recurvirostra americana

L 18" | **WS** 31"

Avocets breed widely but locally in the Columbia Basin, where they are common April–September. They often occur with stilts, but also breed at larger, more alkaline lakes with no vegetation. Like stilts, they nest in the open, and are similarly conspicuous, with loud *pleep pleep pleep* calls from birds flying rapidly overhead as you approach a nesting colony. Although still rare as migrants in western Washington, they are seen there more often than stilts, occasionally in small flocks. Watch for their specialized feeding method, moving quickly through shallow water with the bills scything from side to side, capturing prey by feel.

Large wading shorebird. Upcurved bill, slightly more so in female than male. Black and white plumage; orange on head and neck in breeding plumage replaced by gray in winter. Juvenile also has orange on head and neck.

Black-necked Stilt

Himantopus mexicanus

L 14" | **WS** 29"

First found nesting in the state in 1973, Black-necked Stilts now breed at scattered sites across the Columbia Basin, at shallow, open ponds and lakes with some shore vegetation; they are present April–August. They welcome an intruder to their nesting territory by flying low overhead, long colorful legs dangling, and giving loud, strident *kik-kik-kik* calls. Feeding birds wade up to their bellies; the slender bill is well adapted to capture swimming invertebrates. The four mottled eggs are laid out in the open, so watch for stilts on their nests during incubation. They are seen rarely in migration west, on both fresh and salt water.

Noisy birds of interior ponds. Black and white body, slender black bill, and long bubblegum-pink legs. Male with entirely black back, female brown.

Black-bellied Plover

Pluvialis squatarola

L 11" | **WS** 23"

Black-bellied Plovers are common July–May, with large numbers in both migration and winter. They are easily seen in large bays and estuaries such as Samish Bay, Padilla Bay, and Dungeness Bay, with the largest numbers in Grays Harbor and Willapa Bay and on the open sandy beaches of the nearby outer coast. Their primary prey is large polychaete worms , but during winter high tides, they also feed on earthworms in flooded fields with Dunlins. Much smaller numbers migrate through the Columbia Basin, more in fall than in spring. The plaintive *wheeoreee* calls are a delight to hear.

Our largest plover, with large bill. Breeding male (above) vividly black below and mottled above, with white lower belly and undertail: think of dominos advancing across a mudflat. Female duller above, with much white on underparts. Dark bill and legs. Nonbreeding adult (right) with mottled brown upperparts. Juvenile darker above, breast finely streaked.

American Golden-Plover
Pluvialis dominica

L 10.5" **WS** 26"

Golden-plovers of both species are uncommon to occasionally fairly common fall migrants and rare spring migrants on mudflats and sand beaches on the outer coast, with most records in and around Grays Harbor. A few occur in fall in the Columbia Basin. Small flocks sometimes include both species and, rarely, Black-bellied Plovers. Long-range migrants, both golden-plover species are among the swiftest-flying shorebirds. The flight call of the American is a sharp *queedle*.

Smaller and darker above than Black-bellied, with distinctly smaller bill. Breeding male's (top) underparts entirely black, white neck stripe prominently contrasting. Wings longer, primary feathers project farther than in Pacific. Juvenile (right) brown above, heavily patterned with pale dots. Breast moderately streaked.

Pacific Golden-Plover

Pluvialis fulva

L 10" | **WS** 24"

This beautiful golden-plover is similar in status and habitat preference to the American, but is somewhat more common in fall and much more likely in spring migration. Both species are distinctly less common than a few decades ago. The Pacific's call is a distinctive *tu-wi*.

Bill slightly larger, legs slightly longer than in American Golden-Plover. Breeding male much like American, but white mottling along sides and undertail. Females of both species show more white below.

Wings shorter, primary feathers project less than in American. Juvenile much more yellowish than American especially around head.

Snowy Plover
Charadrius nivosus

L 6" | **WS** 17"

Snowy Plovers are local and uncommon breeders on outer
sand beaches from Grays Harbor south. Leadbetter Point and
the beach from Grayland south are current strongholds, but
human disturbance and the encroachment of introduced beach
grasses threaten these small populations, and the species is
listed as endangered in Washington. Signs are posted to keep
beachgoers aware of breeding birds, which scrape out nest
sites on bare sand near dune vegetation. Breeding adults are
as likely to run when disturbed as to fly. Many birds have been
banded by researchers (as the bird below) to allow close study
of the population. Small numbers remain in the breeding range
in winter. Commonly heard calls are a trilled *purrrrt* and a
whistled *towheet*.

Small, pale plover
of sandy ocean
beaches. Slender
black bill, gray
legs. Breeding
birds with black
head markings
and half-collar.

Nonbreeding birds lack
black markings. Paler than
Semipalmated Plover.

Semipalmated Plover
Charadrius semipalmatus

L 7–7.5" | **WS** 18–20"

These small plovers are common, sometimes abundant, migrants April–May and July–October on outer coastal sand beaches, for example, near Ocean Shores, Westport, Grayland, and Ilwaco. Very small numbers occur as migrants at freshwater locations both west and east. They run and stop to pull four-inch long thin worms from the open sand, stretching them not quite to breaking to extract them and swallowing them quickly. During migration, many also feed on mudflats in coastal bays and estuaries. Small numbers, up to a few dozen at some localities, remain through winter on beaches or even on flooded fields near the coast. Call is a mellow whistled *chuwi*, often given in flight.

Small, dark brown plover with short bill, orange legs Breeding-plumaged male with black markings on head and conspicuous ring on breast, orange-based bill. Brown feathers usually mixed in with black on head of female.

Nonbreeding birds with duller bill, black on head and breast mostly replaced with brown. White eyebrow. Juvenile has pale feather edgings above.

Killdeer

Charadrius vociferus

L 10-11" | **WS** 18-19"

Because they are not restricted to shores, Killdeers are the most ubiquitous of our shorebirds. They breed in open habitats almost everywhere in the lowlands. Common all year west, but the majority in the east withdraw southward in winter. Sparse vegetation and good sightlines are essential for nesting, and nests may be situated in native grassland, pastures, cemeteries, or city parks, and on road shoulders or river sand bars. The adults will let you know when you are too near their nest or young with a spectacular distraction display featuring the rusty rump and tail base. Wintering birds spread out into other open areas, including salt marshes, often gathering into loose flocks. Listen for this species' *tireee tireee* calls, even at night overhead. Males call *killdeer, killdeer* in display flights with slowly beating wings.

Slender plover of upland and water edge. Two black rings on breast, red eye ring, and long tail distinctive. Rusty rump and tail base conspicuous in flight.

Whimbrel
Numenius phaeopus

L 17.5" | **WS** 32"

Whimbrels are common migrants in western Washington, mostly on mud flats and beaches of coastal bays and estuaries. They are considerably more common in spring, when rainfall has created good habitat in flooded fields near the coast, for example, on Camano Island and the Brady Loop Road. Very few are seen in migration east. Occasional birds winter on the coast. This is the most likely of the larger sandpipers to appear on rocky shores. Flight call is a loud *whi-pi-pi-pi-pi*, typically five to seven notes.

Adult. Large sandpiper with smoothly decurved bill more than twice head length. Very plain brown, with dark stripes on head and pale belly. Juvenile has darker back.

Long-billed Curlew

Numenius americanus

L 20-26" | **WS** 25-35"

The striking Long-billed Curlew still breeds locally in eastern Washington grasslands, but as grasslands have declined with the spread of agriculture, so have the curlews. They are early breeders, arriving in mid-March and gone by the end of July. These are our largest sandpipers, the female with a 7-inch-long bill and the male with the bill an inch or two shorter. Small numbers are seen in migration anywhere in the state, and a few remain in winter around Grays Harbor and Willapa Bay. Males on the breeding grounds fly around and around singing *pereee, pereee, pereee* and giving a trilled whistle.

Largest sandpiper, with very long curved bill; male bill one-third shorter than that of female shown here. Rich reddish all over, especially prominent on wings in flight.

Marbled Godwit

Limosa fedoa

L 18" │ **WS** 30"

Marbled Godwits are one of the few shorebirds that have increased in Washington, with up to 1,200 roosting on docks at Westport in recent winters. These are probably from populations breeding in Alaska. More pass along the coast in migration, with larger numbers on the northbound flight April–May than southbound July–September. They roost in large, dense flocks and fly out to forage on beaches and mudflats in Grays Harbor and Willapa Bay, with smaller numbers at Dungeness Bay, probing deep with their long bills. A few are seen in fall migration in the interior, and a few winter at coastal localities. The flight call is reminiscent of the name, a sharp *ga-wit ga-wit.*

Large brown sandpiper, paler below, with long, pink-based bill. Breeding birds have a finely barred breast and darker bill than this non-breeder. Reddish wings distinctive in flight.

Ruddy Turnstone

Arenaria interpres

L 9.5" | **WS** 21"

Brightly marked Ruddy Turnstones pass through our coastal areas in spring, with the largest numbers in and around Grays Harbor. Bottle Beach State Park is a traditional spot for them. Far fewer are seen in fall than spring, as they presumably take a different route southbound. They are very uncommon migrants at freshwater bodies anywhere in the state. This is the starling of the shorebirds, foraging in all situations and eating just about anything, including carrion. They give a low-pitched, musical, rolling chatter as they forage and fly in small flocks.

Short, thick, pointed bill and short, bright orange legs. Breeding male brilliant rusty with black markings above and harlequin head and breast pattern. Female duller, with much brown on head.

Juvenile mottled brown; strong indication of double-U adult breast pattern. Duller legs.

Black Turnstone

Arenaria melanocephala

L 9" | **WS** 21"

Black Turnstones are migrants and winter visitors from tundra breeding grounds in western Alaska, present in Washington from July to May. They always seem busy, running around on coastal rocks and jetties, probing crevices for tiny inverte-brates, and digging barnacles out of their shells with their sharp, pointed bill. They are most common on the wave-washed outer coast, often in mixed flocks with Surfbirds and Rock Sandpipers, but also forage on gravel beaches throughout the Salish Sea. Alki Point, Penn Cove, Neah Bay, and the jetty at Point Brown are all good places for these sandpipers. Their vivid flight pattern and shrill, high-pitched chattering calls make identification straightforward.

Our only small black and white shorebird. Short, pointed bill. Nonbreeding bird with short brown legs. Breeding bird with white patch behind bill, white streaks on breast. Brighter orange-brown legs.

Surfbird
Calidris virgata

L 10" | **WS** 23–26"

This stocky gray sandpiper matches the colors of the rocks it shares with Black Turnstones throughout the winter, from July to early May. Surfbirds can be seen on the coast north of Grays Harbor and throughout the Salish Sea, less commonly to the south. Rocky shorelines, jetties, and breakwaters are good habitat, where the birds jerk mussels right off the rocks with their sharp bill. Good spots include the base of the Point Brown jetty, Neah Bay, Penn Cove, Larabee State Park, and Alki Point in Seattle. Relatively silent, but occasional single high-pitched notes are heard from flocks.

Ploverlike bill, short yellow legs. Black and white tail in flight. Nonbreeding bird with gray upperparts and breast, heart-shaped black spots along sides.

Breeding birds heavily marked all over, with some rust on scapulars.

Red Knot
Calidris canutus

L 10.5" | **WS** 23"

Red Knots are fairly common through most of May at Bottle Beach and Grays Harbor NWR, with up to over 1,000 birds at peak times. The birds roost and feed in dense mixed flocks with Dunlins and Short-billed Dowitchers. Elsewhere on the coast, only small numbers are seen in spring, and similarly small numbers are scattered over a much wider range near protected marine waters from August well into October. East of the Cascades they are very rare at any time. Flight call a musical chirp, sometimes repeated.

Medium-sized, with short, straight bill, dark legs. Breeding bird variably mottled with gray, black, and rusty above; rich reddish below, with white undertail.

Juvenile's upperparts and breast light gray-brown, back and wings finely scalloped white. Legs greenish.

Sanderling
Calidris alba

L 8" | **WS** 17"

Sanderlings are the most common and widespread shorebirds on the sandy beaches of the outer coast. Present in every month, with late northbound migrants and early southbound migrants almost meeting, they occur by the hundreds on long stretches of Pacific beaches, especially on either side of Grays Harbor. Flocks run after receding waves, quickly capturing exposed worms and amphipods, then run back up as the waves advance. They also occur along the rest of the coast in smaller numbers, much less commonly in south Puget Sound. Migrants are widespread in small to moderate numbers east of the Cascades, mostly August–September. Sharp *wick wick* notes are heard from birds feeding or in flight.

Nonbreeding birds are our palest sandpipers, with straight bill, short black legs. Black "wrists" displayed aggressively. Juvenile (left) like nonbreeding adult but with black spangles above. Breeding plumage (not shown), seen briefly in spring, features variably mottled bright orange upperparts and breast; many are less colorful.

Rock Sandpiper

Calidris ptilocnemis

L 9" | **WS** 17"

The best way to see a Rock Sandpiper is to check out flocks of Black Turnstones and Surfbirds from October to early May, as they very often accompany their larger and more conspicuous relatives in probing the seaweed for small mussels, barnacles, and crustaceans. Look for a smaller, longer-billed bird of Surfbird color. The base of the Point Brown jetty has been a good spot. Their numbers are lower away from the outer coast, with few in the Salish Sea. Call a doubled *kerek* or *chereep*, rarely heard.

Juvenile (shown) brown with slender streaked neck, long downward-curved dark bill.

Breeding bird patterned somewhat like Dunlin, but with dark cheek patch, black breast patch farther forward. Legs dark.

Baird's Sandpiper

Calidris bairdii

L 7.5" | **WS** 17"

Most adult Baird's Sandpipers migrate through the Great Plains, so we see mostly juveniles from August to mid-October. Rarely are more than a few seen, with up to two dozen on rare occasions. Much smaller numbers of adults occur in July; there are almost no recent spring records. Numbers are higher east of the Cascades, but they may occur anywhere in the state. More than any other of our shorebirds, they are likely to be seen at high mountain lakes in southward migration, often by glacial tarns. They forage by moving rapidly along the water's edge on both freshwater and marine shores. Flight call a high-pitched, rolling *churrrreep*.

Larger than Semipalmated, Western, or Least, with short, straight bill, black legs. Very long wings project well beyond tail, creating sharply pointed rear end. Juvenile quite buffy, with scalloped upperparts. Breeding adult much less buffy, with more black-marked feathers.

Least Sandpiper

Calidris minutilla

L 6" | **WS** 13"

Least Sandpipers are common migrants late April to mid-May and July–October throughout the state. Much smaller numbers winter coastally, where they may be in flocks totaling low hundreds; wintering birds flock more densely than in migration, but do not join flocks of larger sandpipers such as Dunlins and Western Sandpipers. Leasts usually forage above the zone used by Westerns, at the edge of vegetation or even up among low plants, but these two "peeps," as the smallest sandpipers are called, are often seen together. Quite vocal; flight call a high-pitched *creee-eeep*.

A very small sandpiper with short bill, yellow legs (can be dark if mud-coated). Breeding birds' upperparts with black-centered, rufous-edged feahers. Breast streaked brownish.

Juvenile's upperparts mottled brown and rufous, with fine white lines along back. Breast brownish, finely streaked.

Nonbreeding bird fairly dark plain brown, scapulars with black centers. Only peep with brownish breast in all plumages.

Pectoral Sandpiper

Calidris melanotos

L 9" | **WS** 18"

Pectoral Sandpipers are primarily fall migrants, juveniles coming down from Alaska and even Siberia from July well into October and occurring widely throughout the state in both freshwater and marine habitats. Few are seen in spring, mostly in May. More than most other sandpipers, they forage in small flocks in low vegetation, disappearing among the salicornia in salt marshes. Males are appreciably larger than females. Flight call a low, rolling *chirrrup*.

Yellow-based, slightly droopy bill, yellow legs. Juvenile. richly patterned rusty above, with fine white stripes. Breast brown, with black steaks. Breeding adult duller brown, with little buff, rusty, and white.

Semipalmated Sandpiper

Calidris pusilla

L 6" | **WS** 14"

Semipalmated Sandpipers are uncommon migrants on freshwater and marine shorelines anywhere in the state, much more often seen as fall juveniles August–September than as adults in May or July. They tend to forage a bit higher on the shore than Westerns, but are often seen with them, so look for a shorter-billed, not quite so reddish bird in flocks of Westerns. It is probably easier to find them when there are only a few peeps present at a small pond. Both species have tiny webs between their toes to make mud-walking a bit easier. Flight call a single *chert* or *chut*.

"Peep" with short, thick bill and black legs. Juvenile. brown and black above with reddish or buffy scallops, buffy breast. Breeding-plumaged adult more irregularly marked with black above, more heavily streaked breast.

Western Sandpiper

Calidris mauri

L 6.5" | **WS** 14"

Western is the most abundant sandpiper in Washington during spring migration, when thousands move up the outer coast in late April and early May. Willapa Bay and Grays Harbor are full of them at that time, with large numbers at times on the ocean beaches adjacent to the estuaries. Much smaller numbers stop in similar habitats throughout the Salish Sea, where most forage by probing in shallow water or at shore. Even fewer occur east of the Cascades, where almost all records are from fall, as juveniles scatter away from the coastal migration route. Flight call a high-pitched *dhzeet*.

"Peep" with relatively long bill, black legs. Breeding birds b right rufous on head and scapulars, with heavily streaked underparts. Female, shown here, with particularly long bill.

Juvenile has rufous only in scapulars. Males, shown, with relatively short bill.

Nonbreeding bird plain brown above, finely streaked breast without brown tinge of Least.

Short-billed Dowitcher

Limnodromus griseus

L 11" | **WS** 19"

Short-billed Dowitchers are abundant spring and fairly common fall migrants on the outer coast, especially common at Grays Harbor and Willapa Bay. Bottle Beach from mid-April to early May is the place to see as many as a few thousand in flocks with Dunlins and Western Sandpipers. Hundreds of adults are seen southbound in July all around Grays Harbor, followed by smaller numbers of juveniles; most are gone by the end of September. Elsewhere they occur only in small flocks; they are uncommon away from the coast and rare east of the Cascades. The sharp *tu-tu-tu* calls distinguish them from Long-billed Dowitcher.

Chunky, with long bill, short greenish legs. Breeding plumage heavily patterned above with black, brown, and buff. Mostly reddish below, with fine spots on sides of breast and bars farther back.

Juvenile patterned dark brown and cinnamon above, pale brown to buffy below. Dark tertials with buffy markings. Nonbreeding adults are not seen in Washington.

Long-billed Dowitcher

Limnodromus scolopaceus

L 11.5" | **WS** 19"

As similar as they are, the two dowitcher species are only occasionally found together. Both feed by rapidly probing the mud with their long bills, like living sewing machines. The Long-billed Dowitcher is a bird of fresh water, much more common than Short-billed in that habitat, but especially in the interior, where any shoreline, open or marshy, supports small flocks of Long-billed April–May and July–October. Both spring and fall migration are a bit later than in Short-billed. Still common in fall after the Short-billeds have departed, Long-billeds are the only wintering dowitchers in Washington, mostly near the coast on both freshwater and marine shorelines. Long-billed calls more often than Short-billed, a single or repeated *keek*.

Like Short-billed but bill slightly longer. Breeding birds darker above, with some white-tipped scapulars. Slightly darker and more extensively reddish below, with fine bars on sides of breast and flanks.

Nonbreeding birds plain gray-brown above, mostly white below with barred sides. Juvenile (not shown) like Short-billed but often darker. Tertials virtually unmarked.

Wilson's Snipe

Gallinago delicata

L 10.5" | **WS** 18"

Snipes are regular breeders at marshes and well-vegetated ponds east of the Cascades; they are apparently less common west, where Ridgefield NWR is a good location. They are readily seen when males perch up on fence posts and sing a musical *wicka-wicka-wicka.* power dive with the wings pushing air through the spread outer tail feathers to make a tremolo of louder and louder low, pulsing whistles. They feed by probing the mud in dense marsh vegetation, but often come out into the open while doing so, especially in winter. When flushed they often "tower" upward before heading away, giving a harsh *scaip* or two.

Long bill and short greenish legs. Heavily striped head and upperparts.

Wandering Tattler

Tringa incana

L 10–12" | **WS** 22–26"

Tattlers are rock shorebirds of the outer coast, stopping in May and August–September on their migration to and from California and points south. They are best looked for on jetties, such as at Westport and Ocean Shores, and in small numbers in the Salish Sea; they are only rarely found in Puget Sound. The birds teeter, but less emphatically than Spotted Sandpipers, and usually fly some distance when flushed. The shrill *pi-pi-pi-pi-pi* flight calls are loud enough to be heard over both the crashing of waves and the rushing streams of their breeding habitat.

On rocks. Straight bill, short yellow legs. Breeding plumage gunmetal gray above, heavily barred below. Plain gray in flight.

Juvenile has dusky sides but no bars below, fine pale edges on wing feathers.

Solitary Sandpiper

Tringa solitaria

L 7-9" | **WS** 17-22"

Solitary is the perfect name for this dark sandpiper, almost always seen alone. They occur in a wide variety of freshwater habitats, often associated with woodland, which may explain their habit of "towering," flying straight up and away when flushed. A surprisingly small wooded pond may feature a Solitary Sandpiper, often bobbing the front part of its body up and down. They are present in migration throughout the state, late April to mid-May and July–September. Migrants seem equally common west and east, spring and fall. Solitaries are noisy, with high-pitched three-noted whistles rather like those of Spotted Sandpipers, given as they flush or fly over.

Short bill, somewhat pale at base; medium greenish legs. Prominent white eye ring and finely streaked neck and breast. Bobs forepart of body up and down. Juvenile, shown here, very dark above, dotted with whitish or cinnamon. Breeding adult with larger white spots above and more heavily streaked breast.

Spotted Sandpiper
Actitis macularius

L 7.5" | **WS** 15"

Constantly bobbing their rear end up and down even as downy
chicks, Spotted Sandpipers are common breeders at freshwater
wetlands. They range from lowland rivers and streams to open
and wooded ponds, even storm-water retention ponds, all the
way up to subalpine ponds. Breeding birds require herbaceous
vegetation near shore to shelter their ground nests. Most leave
after breeding, and in migration can be seen at river mouths
and marine habitats, from tidal flats to rock jetties. Small
numbers winter west on freshwater and protected marine
shores. Call high-pitched whistles *peet-weet-weet-weet*,
often in flight.

Short, mostly yellow bill and short pinkish legs. Teeters up and down almost constantly.
Heavily spotted underparts distinctive, males with fewer spots. Nonbreeding and juvenile
have unspotted underparts, with white slash in front of wing.

Lesser Yellowlegs

Tringa flavipes

L 10.5" | **WS** 24"

Lesser Yellowlegs migrate throughout the state; they are less common in spring than in fall, when most seen are juveniles. They walk rapidly through shallow water foraging for invertebrates in freshwater ponds and coastal estuaries, at times "scything" the bill back and forth to find prey by touch, but rarely running like their larger relative. Usually only a few Lessers are seen together; they are just as likely to be in the company of the obviously larger Greaters, when it is easy to distinguish the two. The sharp, double *tu-tu* calls of this species make identification certain, but note the similarity to calls of Short-billed Dowitchers.

Juvenile. Like Greater but smaller. Shorter, straighter bill usually entirely dark.

Greater Yellowlegs

Tringa melanoleuca

L 14" **WS** 28"

This large sandpiper is a common migrant in freshwater and estuarine marine environments. Single birds and small flocks winter in coastal habitats, with migrants arriving throughout the state at the end of March, peaking in April, and trailing off in May. Fall migrants arrive in late June and are common through September, then dwindle to winter numbers. Greaters feed very actively in shallow water, even chasing and catching small fish. Their loud three- or four-note *tew-tew-tew* calls, often given in flight, are attention grabbing.

Juvenile with wings marked with pale dots and notches in dark feathers. Sides unmarked. Bill gray at base. Nonbreeding adult paler brown, with less conspicuous white dots on upperparts.

Longish, very slightly upturned bill. Long neck and long yellow legs. Breeding birds (right) heavily marked black above and on sides.

Wilson's Phalarope

Phalaropus tricolor

L 9" | **WS** 17"

Wilson's Phalaropes are present May–August in freshwater marshes of the interior. They are rare migrants in western Washington, where they have also bred. The larger, more brightly colored females court males, which then incubate the eggs and care for the downy young. Females may then mate with a second male. Usually seen swimming and pecking in the water for prey, the Wilson's is the only phalarope that also commonly forages along the shore, often while running. Short nasal *ernt* calls are given by both sexes.

Male duller than female, with hint of same pattern and white eyebrow.

Juvenile's upperparts dark, all feathers margined buffy. Underparts buffy to white. Legs yellow.

Slender-billed swimming sandpiper, often seen on land. Female with gray crown, black eye line, white throat, black and rusty neck, gray and rusty back. Legs dark.

Red-necked Phalarope

Phalaropus lobatus

L 8" | **WS** 15"

A sandpiper that lands on the ocean is a phalarope. Red-necked Phalaropes are common migrants April–May and July to mid–October off the outer coast, often in small flocks; they are easily seen on pelagic trips from Westport. In fall, flocks of juveniles occur throughout the Salish Sea, where they are often seen from ferries. They are also regular on eastside lakes and ponds, especially in fall. Ocean storms sometimes bring many birds to coastal freshwater ponds, as at Midway Beach. In protected waters, Red-necked Phalaropes feed along convergence lines, where two currents come together and concentrate small crustaceans. Migrants give short, hard *tic* calls when flushed.

Smaller than Wilson's, almost always in water. Female has all-dark head with white eye spot and throat, prominent red slash on neck; upperparts blackish with buffy streaks. Male similar but duller, with white eyebrow.

Juvenile dark above with white and buffy stripes; blackish crown and prominent eye line ("phalarope mark").

Red Phalarope
Phalaropus fulicarius

L 8.5" | **WS** 17"

This most seagoing of the phalaropes is largely confined to offshore waters. Watch for Reds among Red-necked Phalaropes on Westport pelagic trips and from ferries in the Strait of Juan de Fuca. This is the only phalarope that regularly winters at this latitude. From land, they are most often seen in late fall when strong storms blow them to the coast, and are occasionally seen in the Westport marina and even in roadside ponds and ditches. They are also very rare fall migrants on the eastside. As in the other two phalarope species, females are bigger and brighter than males. Rarely heard in migration, the calls are like Red-necked's but slightly higher-pitched and more musical.

Female has short, black-tipped yellow bill. Head black with white cheeks. Striped black and cream above, entirely rusty red below. Male much duller, with brown crown and white eyebrow; may be mostly whitish below.

Nonbreeding adult gull-gray above, dark phalarope mark through eye. Short, thick black bill. Juvenile with more prominently striped back.

Pomarine Jaeger

Stercorarius pomarinus

L 23" | **WS** 52"

Jaegers are pirates, harassing other seabirds to steal their fish. The targets of the Pomarine's kleptoparasitism include birds as large as Pink-footed Shearwaters and Sabine's and California Gulls . This species is common offshore in May and July–October; they are much less often seen from shore, but small numbers have occurred throughout the Salish Sea, well into Puget Sound. This is the only jaeger species to winter off Washington, though in small numbers.

Bulky jaeger with extensively pale flight feathers. Adult's longer central tail feathers wide and blunt-tipped. Breast often mottled black.

Parasitic Jaeger

Stercorarius parasiticus

L 20" | **WS** 46"

The Parasitic is the most widespread jaeger in Washington, seen not only offshore but from land all along the coast. Once common in protected waters of the Salish Sea September–October, they have become much less so with the massive decline of Common Terns in the region. The primary targets of their kleptoparasitism are now Bonaparte's Gulls. Fall records in the interior are concentrated at Potholes Reservoir, Sprague Lake, and the Walla Walla River delta on the Columbia River.

Adult dark above with black cap, white below, with pale breast band, dark wing linings, and dark undertail. Short, pointed central tail feathers.

Juvenile heavily barred all over. Central tail feathers pointed, barely longer than rest of tail.

Long-tailed Jaeger

Stercorarius longicaudus

L 15-23" | **WS** 40-46"

Long-tailed Jaegers get many of their fish from Arctic Terns. They are the least common of the three jaegers, rarely seen in May and usually in only small numbers August–September, but fortunate observers have seen more than 100 on some Westport pelagic trips. Occasional birds, mostly immatures, have been seen in fall in the Salish Sea and, more rarely, on reservoirs and rivers east of the Cascades, where there are even a few June records.

Adult has very long, pointed central tail feathers. Whiter breast and more gray on belly than Parasitic. Juvenile distinguished from Parasitic by smaller size, blunt-tipped central tail feathers, and grayer coloration.

Common Murre

Uria aalge

L 17.5" | **WS** 26"

Small numbers of Common Murres breed on islands from
Tatoosh to Point Grenville, then vacate those islands in
postbreeding dispersal, when each male takes its single chick
to sea. These pairs are frequently seen on offshore boat trips.
Many birds that have bred between Alaska and Oregon enter
Washington's productive waters and spread east to Admiralty
Inlet, with far fewer in Puget Sound. Murres are heard giving
their low, persistent *murr murr murr* at the breeding islands,
and when counter-calling with their much higher-voiced
offspring at sea.

All alcids dive and swim underwater with relatively small wings and have compact bodies
and short necks. This species has a heavy, pointed bill. Breeding bird dark brown-black
above and white below, with dark streaks on sides.

Nonbreeding plumage with
neck and underparts white;
black streak behind eye.

Pigeon Guillemot
Cepphus columba

L 13.5" | **WS** 23"

Pigeon Guillemots nest locally but sometimes abundantly in burrows and crevices on islands and coastal mainland slopes from Point Grenville north, a few at jetties farther south. The San Juan Islands and Protection Island have the largest populations. Some pairs use protected crevices in docks and piers, even the Hood Canal Bridge, as nest sites. At breeding sites you can see parents continually bringing fish such as sculpins and gunnels to their two chicks. After the chicks fledge, they occupy all Salish Sea waters, with small numbers on the outer coast. Adults are very vocal in the breeding season, both members of the pair giving high-pitched trilled whistles several seconds long.

Smaller than murre, with smaller bill. Breeding adult all black except for big white wing patches, red feet and mouth lining.

Nonbreeding birds variable, black feathers replaced largely by white; wing patches still present. The palest alcid in winter.

Marbled Murrelet

Brachyramphus marmoratus

L 10" | **WS** 16"

Marbled Murrelets lay their single egg in a nest high in a large conifer in old-growth forests as far as 50 miles inland, and fly out to sea to forage on small fish. They pair for life and are separated only when one is at the nest; two small alcids keeping close together is a good indication that they are of this species. Diving and feeding adults keep in touch with high-pitched whistled *keer* calls; those calls heard over coastal forests help researchers find the nests. Common decades ago, this species has declined greatly with the loss of old-growth nesting forests and declines in fish populations. It is now considered endangered in Washington, but a few can be seen anywhere in the Salish Sea.

Very small, with tiny, thin bill. Breeding birds entirely dark brown, like a wren of the sea.

Usually in pairs. Nonbreeding birds black above, white below. White half-collar and scapular streak.

Ancient Murrelet

Synthliboramphus antiquus

L 10" | **WS** 17"

This little gray-backed alcid is usually seen in small flocks on the Salish Sea beginning in November. They range widely, especially in areas of rapid currents, along the Strait of Juan de Fuca east to Admiralty Inlet; Point Wilson and Point No Point are both good sites. Individuals and entire flocks dive suddenly from rapid low flight straight into the water, a characteristic of this species. Numbers usually remain high through January, then just as suddenly the flocks disappear. On the outer coast, birds are present through much of the year, though least common in fall, and a few may breed on offshore islands.

Slightly larger than Marbled Murrelet, with thicker, pale bill. Nonbreeding plumage with black head and gray back

Cassin's Auklet

Ptychoramphus aleuticus

L 9" | **WS** 15"

These tiny seabirds are at home well offshore, where they dive at night for krill and other crustaceans that they carry back to their nesting burrow in special throat pouches. They breed on forested rocks off the northern outer coast, and fly dozens of miles farther out to feed. Numbers are highest September–October, when migrants from farther north pass through. Most birds are out at sea after breeding. Most of those seen in the Salish Sea, all the way down into Puget Sound, are probably failed breeders or birds displaced by poor feeding conditions, especially in El Niño years.

Entirely dark gray, paler below, with white spot above eye. Bill short and relatively thick.

Rhinoceros Auklet
Cerorhinca monocerata

L 15" | **WS** 22"

One of the largest breeding colonies, with approximately 36,000 pairs, of this chunky brown seabird is on Protection Island. Other colonies include Destruction Island on the outer coast. The single egg is laid in a burrow the pair has dug, and the adults come and go at night to avoid predation by gulls. Schooling fish, especially sand lance, are their primary prey. After breeding, they disperse to the open ocean, sometimes in small flocks, with many coming into Puget Sound for the winter, where they sometims give close views just off fishing piers. Silent at sea, they give a great variety of low-pitched calls at the burrow.

Short-necked and brown to the waterline; easily recognized in breeding plumage by the facial plumes and "horn" at bill base.

Nonbreeding birds in winter lack plumes and "horn." Watch them open their wings as they dive.

Tufted Puffin

Fratercula cirrhata

L 15" | **WS** 25"

Outrageous-looking Tufted Puffins nest in burrows on coastal islands from Point Grenville north to Tatoosh and in the Strait of Juan de Fuca east to Protection and Smith Islands. After breeding, they retire to the open ocean, mostly south of Washington. Regularly scheduled summer boat trips around Protection Island offer a chance to see puffins, or you can scope Tatoosh Island from Cape Flattery and perhaps see a few flying around the island or near their burrows. Westport pelagic trips are a third opportunity. Only rarely are they seen in protected waters south of Admiralty Inlet.

Breeding birds black, with big orange bill, white face, and showy golden plumes.

Black-legged Kittiwake

Rissa tridactyla

L 17" | **WS** 36"

Kittiwakes are primarily winter visitors mid–September to
mid–May to the outer Washington coast. Although preferring
offshore waters, where they drop to the surface to capture
small fishes and squids, they can sometimes be seen from shore.
Look for them at the Grays Harbor jetties, flying past Cape
Flattery, and at Neah Bay, where they sometimes join roosting
gull flocks. Immatures very rarely appear at eastside lakes in
late fall. They prefer to roost on rocks if they can find them. In
flight, the choppy wing beat helps distinguish them from other
gulls. The *kit-i-wak* call, so prominent at breeding colonies, is
rarely heard in Washington waters.

Small gull with dark eyes
and plain yellow, somewhat
arched bill. Black legs.
Adults with restricted solid
black wing tips.

Immature with black ear
spot and hindneck bar. Black
line along wing coverts and
black tail tip. Attains adult
plumage in three years.

Sabine's Gull

Xema sabini

L 13.5" | **WS** 33"

Our only gulls with a slightly forked tail, Sabine's are tern-like in flight, often well above the water, and are mostly seen in offshore waters. They are common migrants April–May and August–September as they pass between Arctic breeding grounds and the productive waters of the Humboldt Current. They are commonly seen on Westport pelagic trips, and are even more abundant over the Swiftsure Bank between Washington and British Columbia, which is also occasionally visited by pelagic trips. They are also rare fall visitors on reservoirs east. The highly patterned wings are distinctive even at great distance.

Small pelagic gull. Each wing divided into gray, white, and black panels. Breeding bird with black head and yellow-tipped black bill. Juvenile brown above, with black-scalloped back and wings. Wing pattern in flight otherwise as in adult. Matures in two years.

Bonaparte's Gull
Chroicocephalus philadelphia

L 13.5"   **WS** 33"

Bonaparte's Gulls are ternlike in flight, not much larger than
the Common Terns with which they sometimes associate. Large
numbers migrate through the Salish Sea April–May and again
from late July to early November; fewer are on the outer coast,
with only small numbers at freshwater bodies in the interior
both spring and fall. Smaller numbers spend the winter on
the Salish Sea. They often dip to the surface to feed in swift-
running currents, as at Point No Point, even in very large flocks.
From a distance, flocks look like silver confetti scattered over
the water. Calls are harsh and ternlike.

Very small gull with black bill, red feet. Primaries
mostly white with black tips. Breeding adult with black
head.

First-year bird with black ear spot and tail tip.
Patterned wings, with dark front and rear edges,
brown bar across coverts. Matures in two years.

Heermann's Gull

Larus heermanni

L 18-21"   **WS** 45-51"

From their breeding islands in the Gulf of California, large numbers of these very distinctive gulls migrate to Washington in late June and July, arriving with the white heads of breeding plumage. They quickly begin to molt and become gray-headed, assuming their "winter" plumage in August, then stay into early November. They are common all along the coast, roosting alongside other gulls but almost always in their own dense flocks. They move into the Salish Sea later in summer and become common down to Puget Sound. Up to 1,000 have roosted on the breakwater at the Edmonds fishing pier in fall. The chocolate-brown immatures stay on the outer coast. Calls are harsher than those of most other gulls.

Nonbreeding adult dark gray, with paler head; black-tipped red bill and black legs.

First-year birds unmarked dark chocolate brown with black-tipped pinkish bill. Matures in three years.

Mew Gull

Larus canus

L 16" | **WS** 43"

After the Glaucous-winged, the much smaller Mew is the most common wintering gull in the Salish Sea, from August to early May. Mew Gulls are somewhat less common on the outer coast, where they usually stay within sight of land. They often feed at convergence lines, where two currents come together. They hover in place with feet paddling the surface while picking up small fish and crustaceans. The obvious large white spots in the black wing tip distinguish adults from other species. The call really does sound something like the cat's meow.

Small, round-headed gull with sma[ll] bill, dark eyes, and yellow legs. Adu[lt] with yellow bill and large white spo[ts] in black wing tips. Head smudged gray in nonbreeding plumage. First-year bird (left) light brown, like coffee with cream; primaries and t[ail] darker. Bill pink at base. Mantle becomes gray during first winter. Matures in three years.

Ring-billed Gull

Larus delawarensis

L 17.5" | **WS** 48"

Ring-billed Gulls have adapted very well to humans, often begging handouts in parking lots or feeding on lawns. They are generally freshwater birds, breeding on islands in large lakes in the Columbia Basin and along the Columbia River down to East Sand Island. Most leave the lakes in winter, but many remain on the river, and they are also widespread on lakes throughout the western lowlands. They also inhabit salt water and are common residents in Grays Harbor, with small numbers nesting on islands there. All larger gulls go through a ring-billed stage as they mature, but they don't have the yellow legs of adults of this species. Calls are lower-pitched than those of larger gulls.

Medium-sized gull with pale mantle, extensively black wing tips. Breeding adult's bill yellow with black ring, eyes and legs yellow. Head streaked in nonbreeding plumage.

First-year birds with bright pink bill base and pink feet. Wing coverts pale, relatively lightly patterned. Gray mantle appears in first winter. Matures in three years.

Western Gull

Larus occidentalis

L 25" | **WS** 58"

Large, large-billed, and dark-mantled, Westerns are the gulls of the outer coast, breeding on most offshore islands and on islands in Grays Harbor. They are resident through the year, restricted to salt water except for occasional wandering up the Columbia River. Identical to Glaucous-winged in habits, Westerns far outnumber them on the outer coast, but the two species interbreed widely. Their hybrids, exhibiting every degree of intermediate appearance from dark to light, are widespread in the Salish Sea in winter, where these confusing gulls are easily seen in roosting flocks along with much smaller numbers of pure Westerns.

Large, dark-mantled gull with heavy bill, black wing tips, pink legs. Adult's bill yellow with red spot. Head remains white in nonbreeding plumage.

First-year birds heavily patterned and dark all over, with black bill and dull pinkish legs. Matures in four years.

California Gull

Larus californicus

L 21" | **WS** 54"

California Gulls breed on islands with Ring-billed on Columbia Basin lakes and Columbia River islands, then largely migrate out of the state in winter; many cross to the westside before leaving. Look for them migrating down the Columbia River and over the Cascades. Their numbers are augmented by thousands from breeding colonies in Canada, and they are widely distributed and abundant July–October, when they are the most common gull on the outer coast, with large numbers offshore. Small numbers remain to winter. Some immatures, scraggly in molt, remain in the western lowlands through the summer. Calls are lower-pitched than those of larger gulls.

Breeding adult with dark eyes, yellow bill with both red and black spot. Mantle darker than in Ring-billed. Head streaked and legs greenish in nonbreeding birds.

First-year bird medium-sized, mottled brown, with extensive pink on bill base. Matures in four years.

Herring Gull

Larus argentatus

L 25" | **WS** 58"

Common in much of the northern hemisphere, in Washington Herring Gulls are less common than Glaucous-winged, Western, and California Gulls, except in the interior in winter. They are visitors all across the state September–April, mostly on lakes and rivers and along the outer coast, with fewer in the Salish Sea. The bill is not as heavy as in the slightly larger Glaucous-winged and Western Gulls. Brown immatures in flight have secondaries paler than primaries. The calls are like those of other large gulls.

Large gull with black wing tips contrasting with pale mantle. Eyes pale yellow, bill yellow with red spot. Nonbreeding adult's head streaked; entirely white in breeding birds. Matures in four years.

Iceland Gull

Larus glaucoides

L 23" | **WS** 55"

Iceland Gulls, formerly known as Thayer's Gulls on the Pacific Coast, are widespread in small numbers on large freshwater lakes and at coastal beaches and estuaries September–April, as common in the Salish Sea as on the outer coast. They forage over the water and roost with other large gulls, as at the Elwha River mouth. All ages are pink-legged, with round heads and relatively small bills, rather more gentle-looking than the other large gulls. The wing tips are much darker above than below in all plumages. Adult eye color is pale or dark.

Large gull with small bill, rounded head. Nonbreeding adult with pale mantle, red-spotted yellow bill, and pink legs like Herring, but less black in wing tips, very little showing from below. Eyes brown to yellowish.

First-year bird resembles immature Glaucous-winged, but bill small. Wing tips black above, paler below. Matures in four years.

Glaucous-winged Gull

Larus glaucescens

L 26" | **WS** 58"

These are the quintessential large gulls of the Salish Sea, the baseline species for comparison with other gulls. Present all year, they breed on many islands throughout the region, and some pairs take advantage of docks, piers, and roofs as nest sites. Small numbers also wander up the Columbia River into the interior. Young birds wear a different plumage in each of the four years they take to reach maturity, a range of variation that can challenge beginners but delights gull-lovers. Adult Glaucous-wings are large, with a pale mantle and slightly darker wing tips, pink legs, and yellow bill with red spot. This species hybridizes with Westerns, producing young of intermediate appearance. The calls are loud and varied, the music of the coast.

Large, with pale mantle, wing tips not much darker. Adults have brown eyes, yellow bill with red spot. Legs pink. Head variably mottled with gray in winter.

First-year bird coffee-and-cream brown all over. Bill black, legs dull pinkish.

Second year. Body with much white, back feathers gray; some gray in wing. Bill developing some pale color.

Third year. Rather like nonbreeding adult with mostly gray wings, but some darker color in wings and wingtips with smaller white spots. Tail with much gray. Bill mixed yellow and black, sometimes with partial red spot.

Caspian Tern

Hydroprogne caspia

L 21" | **WS** 50"

The largest Caspian Tern colony in the world is on East Sand Island in the Lower Columbia River, with smaller colonies upriver on Goose and Crescent Islands. Other colonies in Grays Harbor and the Salish Sea have waxed and waned. A few birds can be seen on larger water bodies anywhere in the state, in search of feeding and perhaps new nesting areas. They dive from high above the water for fish of all kinds, which they swallow in the air or carry back to the nest. The calls are loud and harsh, high-pitched in juveniles and raspy in adults.

Largest tern in the world, with big, bright red bill. Upper surface of wings flashes silvery in sun, lower surfaces of primaries black. Breeding adult with extensive black cap; some white in forecrown in nonbreeding plumage.

Common Tern

Sterna hirundo

L 12" | **WS** 30"

Common Terns are uncommon migrants mid-April to May and July–October in coastal Washington, occasionally common on the outer coast. They have declined dramatically in the Salish Sea, for unknown reasons. East of the Cascades they are uncommon in fall, mostly September, at lakes and larger rivers. They often occur in tight flocks. They roost on beaches, and often associate with Bonaparte's Gulls in the Salish Sea. Calls are a loud *tee-arrrr* and repeated *kik-kik-kik*.

Small tern with long, pointed wings and long, forked tail. Short, red-orange legs. Breeding adult has black cap, black-tipped orange bill. Nonbreeding plumage with white forehead. Immature with dark bill and dark bar along front edge of wing.

Arctic Tern

Sterna paradisaea

L 12" | **WS** 31"

To see Arctic Terns, take a pelagic trip out of Westport, where they are commonly seen in late May and from mid-August to mid-September. Scattered birds, occasionally small flocks, fly gracefully well above the water, apart from the masses of shearwaters and gulls at the fishing boats. The bill and neck are shorter than in Common Terns, and both adults and immature Arctics look whiter, with fewer dark markings. They are rare migrants anywhere else in the state, but records are widespread, usually of birds in flight over a lake. They have even bred a few times at Dungeness and Everett. Alarm call is *tee-arrrr*, higher-pitched than that of Common and rarely heard in Washington.

In breeding plumage similar to Common, but bill entirely red, underparts grayer, legs even shorter. Nonbreeding and immature with white forehead, dark bill.

Forster's Tern

Sterna forsteri

L 13" | **WS** 31"

Forster's Terns, their wings flashing silver, occur in the Columbia Basin May to mid-September, breeding at a few lakes and probably on reservoirs along the Columbia River, with the largest population at the Potholes Reservoir. They nest on small islands and on flattened marsh vegetation. After breeding, they are seen at other eastern Washington wetlands, then head south to California and Mexico. They are very rare migrants in western Washington, usually seen over salt water. Alarm calls are much like those of Common Tern.

Like Common, but slightly longer-billed and longer-tailed, wings more silvery above. Nonbreeding birds have black restricted to sides of head.

Black Tern

Chlidonias niger

L 9-10" | **WS** 22-24"

Small numbers of Black Terns nest on wooded lakes and ponds in northeastern Washington, from Okanogan County east. Single birds turn up in migration throughout the interior and more sparingly at lakes and sewage lagoons in the western lowlands. Their dark coloration makes them harder to see than white terns, especially when perched in the marsh vegetation where they nest. They are noisy on the breeding grounds, with sharp *kik kik ki*k calls. Birds in nonbreeding plumage are much grayer on the back than other terns.

Small tern, all gray above, with shorter tail than other small terns. In breeding plumage, head and underparts black, undertail white. Nonbreeding adult and immature gray above, white below.

Red-throated Loon
Gavia stellata

L 25" | **WS** 36"

These small, pale loons with an uptilted bill are widespread
along the Washington coast from mid-September to early May;
the dull red of the throat may be visible in late spring. A good
place to see them is West Beach in Deception Pass State Park
as individuals and small flocks fly in through the pass on the
outgoing tide, only to land and be carried back out by the swift
current as they forage for small schooling fish. Large numbers
are occasionally seen along the outer coast in northbound and
southbound migrations. They are also often seen near shore,
hunting for bottom fish. This and the Pacific Loon are silent
while in our waters.

Small loon with thin, uptilted
bill. Breeding adult has gray
head and dull reddish foreneck,
plain back with fine lines.

Neck extensively white
in nonbreeding adult,
duskier in immature.

Common Loon
Gavia immer

L 32" | **WS** 46"

Common Loons nest in small numbers on many lakes in the
northern half of the state, mostly east of the Cascades, and
migrate to coastal locations and larger bodies of freshwater
in winter. Adults arrive on the coast in late August, then
spread out across large bays to hunt for bottom fish and crabs;
numbers increase when juveniles follow, making this the most
common loon in Puget Sound. Common Loons are our largest
seabirds, dwarfing the other loons, grebes, and cormorants that
feed in the same places. They are well known on the breeding
grounds for their wailing calls, which are also heard in April as
wintering birds prepare to migrate.

Large loon with huge spearlike bill.
Breeding adult with iridescent black
head and white "necklace." White
markings scattered across upperparts.

Head shape often angular. Nonbreeding
birds with large pale bill, dark hindneck with
white notches intruding from white foreneck.
Immature with pale scallops on back.

Pacific Loon

Gavia pacifica

L 23-29" | **WS** 43-50"

Watch for Pacific Loons where currents are swift and schooling fish are so abundant that dozens or even hundreds of loons assemble to hunt them. Large numbers are present on the outer coast in May and October, when almost the entire population migrates up and down our coast, and many winter in the western and northern parts of the Salish Sea. Small numbers are seen on large rivers and reservoirs east, especially in fall migration.

Small loon with puffy gray head, slender pointed bill held parallel to water. In breeding plumage, neck with lines on sides, iridescent green (black at distance) in front. White markings on back form discrete patches.

Nonbreeding birds dark brown above; smooth straight line between dark hindneck and white foreneck. Adult with "chin strap," lacking in immature.

Black-footed Albatross

Phoebastria nigripes

L 32" | **WS** 84"

The excitement is palpable when the first of these big, long-winged travelers is spotted on a pelagic trip out of Westport, about the only way to see them. They are present all year, but numbers peak from late April to mid-October, when dozens can be seen at fishing boats over Grays Canyon, off Grays Harbor. They are often first seen at a distance, but chumming—tossing oil, suet, and herring from the boat—can bring them thrillingly close. With their goose-like size and seven-foot wingspan, albatrosses are unmistakable.

Large, brown pelagic bird with long, narrow wings, gliding over the ocean with scarcely a wingbeat. Somewhat gooselike, but with large hooked bill, tubular nostrils. Adults have whitish face.

Sooty Shearwater

Ardenna grisea

L 17" | **WS** 40"

Sooty Shearwaters from New Zealand breeding colonies assemble by the thousands off the Washington coast, mostly April–October. They can be abundant on pelagic trips, where you can see them at close range making shallow dives into the water for prey, but tens of thousands can also be seen from shore as they pass coastal viewing points such as Ocean Shores and Westport. Sometimes they are heading north at a rate of a dozen per second, creating one of Washington's true wildlife spectacles. Watch for dark, gull-sized birds with a silvery flash on the underwing as they rise up on the breeze, alternating stiff-winged flaps and glides. They also rest on the water, sometimes in dense flocks.

hearwaters give a few steady flaps,
hen glide for a long distance. This
pecies is all dark, with underside of
ings contrasting white. Small, dark
hearwater with slender hooked
ill. California Gull size.

Leach's Storm-Petrel

Hydrobates leucorhous

L 8" | **WS** 20"

At last count, 50,000 Leach's Storm-Petrels nest in Washington, ten times as many as Fork-tailed, on twice as many islands, but because Leach's forage in warm water much farther offshore, they are seen much less often. They are at the nesting islands May-August, then mostly disappear from Washington waters; occasional winter storms, however, bring a few of both storm-petrels close to shore, even far into the Salish Sea. Chattering and purring calls are given by both sexes at the colony.

Small, dark pelagic bird with big white rump patch, erratic flight.

Fork-tailed Storm-Petrel

Hydrobates furcatus

L 8.5" | **WS** 19"

Weighing just two ounces, storm-petrels are surprisingly small birds to spend most of their life at sea as they do. Fork-tails nest in colonies on Carroll, Bodelteh, Tatoosh, and Alexander Islands, off the northern outer coast, where they come and go at night to avoid predation by gulls. The fish and crustaceans the adults catch and eat are digested to produce oil, which is then fed to the single chick in a two-foot-long burrow. The chick is especially fluffy to help conserve body warmth when both parents are away on long foraging trips. Both sexes give a raspy 3- to 5-note call at the colony.

Small, gray pelagic bird with forked tail, rather steady flight.

Northern Fulmar

Fulmarus glacialis

L 18" | **WS** 42"

Fulmars come to us from breeding islands in and around the Bering Sea and Gulf of Alaska. They are common throughout the year in Washington, as many immatures are present in the state all summer, and the adults visit us as soon as they vacate their breeding cliffs. They are commonly seen on pelagic trips off Westport, when they may fly right up to the boat as they squabble over chum. Much more rarely, they are seen from shore or in the Salish Sea, such as from the west coast of Whidbey Island or Point No Point. They vary from gull-colored to entirely dark gray, and can be distinguished from shearwaters by the choppy flight style and short, thick, yellow bill held downward.

Light-morph birds have gull-like plumage but thick, tube-nosed bill. Tail and wings gray. Steady flapping alternates with gliding.

Dark-morph birds, more common in Washington than light, are gray all over. Some individuals are intermediate.

Pelagic Cormorant

Phalacrocorax pelagicus

L 28" | **WS** 39"

This smallest of our cormorants is ubiquitous in marine waters, nesting widely on both islands and mainland wherever there are cliff ledges. Pelagic Cormorants also nest on human structures, such as under a bridge in Bremerton and at the ferry dock in Anacortes. Notwithstanding the name "pelagic," meaning "out at sea," this species stays near shore to feed on bottom creatures such as gunnels, sculpins, and shrimp. The ornamental paired crests and white thigh patches are attained in February, then lost while nesting in July. Groans, grunts, and hisses are heard at nesting colonies.

Very slender bill, with hook scarcely evident. Adult iridescent dark purple and green. White flanks, red face, and wispy fore-and-aft crests in breeding birds.

Slender, straight neck in flight; small bill. Obviously long-tailed. Immature dark all over.

Double-crested Cormorant

Phalacrocorax auritus

L 33" | **WS** 52"

Double-crested Cormorants can be seen throughout the state on water bodies large and small, fresh and salt. Breeding colonies, often shared with Great Blue Herons, are widespread in the interior. While most interior birds depart for the winter, cormorants are ubiquitous all year in coastal waters, breeding from rocky islands in the Salish Sea to East Sand Island in the Lower Columbia, the largest known colony. They eat bottom fish such as sculpins, catching them while propelled themselves underwater with their big webbed feet. As predators of young salmon and trout, cormorants have been endlessly persecuted by wildlife agencies, yet the species continues to thrive. Birds at nesting colonies make grunting calls.

Neck thick, somewhat kinked in flight. Immature with pale bill and face; neck and breast become darker with age.

Upperparts brown and scal looking. Adult with pale bill, face and throat skin orange Eyes bright green. Paired white or black head plumes in breeding season.

Brandt's Cormorant

Phalacrocorax penicillatus

L 34" | **WS** 48"

Brandt's Cormorants are easily seen on the outer coast as thousands migrate into Washington from California and Oregon; they spend the winter here and then return south in spring, a direction opposite to the prevailing migration of most other species. They feed on schooling fish in deep channels, often in association with loons and alcids. They roost on rocks and on dock pilings at ferry landings throughout the Salish Sea, developing their breeding colors in early spring. There are nesting colonies on coastal cliffs at a few outer-coast localities such as Destruction Island, Willoughby Rock, Cape Disappointment, and East Sand Island.

Head rounded, bill long and slender. Adult shiny black with buff patches at bill base. Blue eyes. White plumes develop in March, when bare throat skin turns blue.

Straight neck in flight, relatively short tail. Immature blackish above, brown below. Buff face patch sometimes visible.

American White Pelican

Pelecanus erythrorhynchos

L 62" | **WS** 108"

Once gone from Washington as a breeding species, several thousand of these huge, showy birds now nest on Badger Island in the Columbia River and wander far and wide into the Columbia Basin, where there are also many nonbreeding birds. Watch the sky, as pelicans spend much time high in the air between their feeding and roosting areas. Check the Yakima River at Horn Rapids Park, where they capture fish coming over the low dam. In recent years, more and more have been turning up west of the Cascades, for example, at Deer Lagoon on Whidbey Island. They feed while swimming, often advancing in a line to herd fish into their wide-open bills.

Usually on fresh water. Very large, with huge, pouched yellow bill; slight crest. All white with black primaries, often seen high in air. Vertical plate on bill grown during breeding, then shed.

Brown Pelican

Pelecanus occidentalis

L 51" | **WS** 79"

One of the spectacular sights of the outer coast is a group of Brown Pelicans diving from the air to capture schooling fish. This species is a conservation success story, once endangered by DDT and other pesticides in their prey, but now common along much of the west coast. After breeding in southern California and Mexico, thousands migrate to our outer coast mid–April to October, where they can be seen fishing and roosting in Grays Harbor and on the Lower Columbia River. As many as 16,000 have been reported roosting on East Sand Island in the Lower Columbia. A few wander into the Salish Sea.

Adult light gray-brown with white head and neck; neck largely dark brown in breeding. Narrower bill and wings than American White Pelican.

Saltwater pelican with long bill and expansible pouch. Immature brown above, white below, with dull head, bill, and pouch.

American Bittern

Botaurus lentiginosus

L 28" | **WS** 42"

Bitterns are marsh herons resting in tall marsh vegetation and remaining hidden until one flies up in front of you or suddenly steps into the open at the edge of the cattails. They sometimes stand with the bill pointing straight up to blend in with the vegetation even better. They are present only April to mid-November east; in the west, especially southwest, very small numbers also regularly winter. Bitterns are well known for their loud *oong-ka-choonk* calls in spring .

Wading bird of freshwater marshes, with pointed bill, medium-length greenish legs. Beautifully camouflaged with barring and striping.

Great Blue Heron

Ardea herodias

L 46" | **WS** 72"

Great Blue Herons are common residents throughout the state, conspicuous almost everywhere at the waterside, both fresh and salt. They feed mostly in estuaries at low tide, then retire to roost at high tide, often in trees. The very conspicuous nesting colonies, known as heronries, are in groves of medium to tall trees near the water. They feed on fish of all kinds, some surprisingly large, and also take snakes, amphibians, and even birds. In winter, many resort to hunting voles in fields, often with good success. They can be distinguished in flight by the bowed wings, almost as wide as an eagle's, and the neck pulled in against the back. Call is a loud, croaking *graaahnk*, often as a bird flushes.

Long-legged, long-necked wading bird with long, pointed yellow bill, reddish legs. Adult has white head with black head stripe, reddish neck and thighs, gray body with some black markings. Head and neck plumes longest during breeding.

Neck retracted during flight on bowed wings. Dark flight feathers contrast with gray body. Immature with dark crown.

Great Egret

Ardea alba

L 39" | **WS** 51"

Once rare in Washington, these showy white birds began to breed at the north end of the Potholes Reservoir in 1979. While that remains the primary breeding colony, birds are now seen all over the Columbia Basin April-September and in southwest Washington July-September, perhaps dispersing from colonies farther south. Their diet is much like that of the Great Blue Heron, even stalking voles on land at times. Watch for developing plumes as breeding season begins. Calls are high-pitched croaks, not as startling as those of Great Blue Herons.

All white, with yellow bill and black legs. Smaller than Great Blue Heron, but similar flight style. Lores turn green during breeding, when long display plumes are grown.

Green Heron

Butorides virescens

L 18" | **WS** 26"

Green Herons are accomplished fisherbirds, even using small edible items as bait to attract their unsuspecting prey. Rather than wading, they fish from shore, or perch on floating vegetation or low branches overhanging the water. They are summer visitors in Washington May–September, largely restricted to the westside; they are scarce there in winter, and even scarcer east. A good way to see them is by kayaking or canoeing the Black River south of Olympia. Isolated pairs nest in shrubs on the edges of wooded lakes, ponds, and streams. When flushed, these little herons utter a loud *kyow*, startling and distinctive. In flight, they are dark and crow-sized, but the bowed wings and legs extending behind the tail are distinctive.

Small, compact heron with black bill, yellow legs. Dark glossy greenish above, paler below. Purple-chestnut on neck and breast. Black cap and white neck stripe. Immature heavily streaked below. Perches above water.

Black-crowned Night-Heron

Nycticorax nycticorax

L 25" | **WS** 44"

Night-herons are denizens of lakes and ponds in the
interior May–September; small numbers still occur widely
in the Columbia Basin, but the species is experiencing a
continuing decline. Very few stay to winter. Feeding at night,
they can often be seen roosting in willows or on canal banks
during the day. When they flush or fly around, they give single
low-pitched *wok* calls, a good indication of their presence at
night. Their eyes are very large, an adaptation for night feeding.

Compact, medium-sized heron with relatively short
bill and legs. Adult gray and white with black crown
and back, white head plumes, red eyes. Subadult
with gray underparts, no plume. Immature (left)
somewhat bitternlike, but much shorter neck,
more simply patterned in brown and white. Eyes orange.
Not found in dense marsh vegetation.

Turkey Vulture

Cathartes aura

L 26" | **WS** 67"

Turkey Vultures are widespread in the state from late March to October; numbers have increased in recent years. They breed locally, usually on ledges or in cliff crevices, but range far and wide to search for carrion. They can be recognized as they sail overhead by the angle of their wings, each wing raised above the horizontal. When a breath of wind destabilizes the bird, first one wing and then the other shifts to the horizontal, increasing lift. Not often seen feeding on roadkill, they find most of their carrion elsewhere, led by their great sense of smell to dead animals as small as mice. Large numbers migrate past Cape Flattery April–May and across the Strait of Juan de Fuca September–October.

Long-winged, eagle-like soaring bird. Black, with two-toned wings, plain tail, small red head. Flies with wings held above horizontal.

Distinctly smaller than eagles, with small, mostly naked red head and long bill. Much brown above. Legs pinkish.

Osprey
Pandion haliaetus

L 23" | **WS** 63"

These long-winged fishing hawks are easily recognized by
the pronounced crook in their wings as they soar over the
water. Watch long enough, and one will drop from the sky
with impressive talons extended to come up with a large fish.
Their numbers have increased greatly after a population crash
caused by DDT. They occur near water throughout Washington
mid–March through October, occasionally wintering. They
probably nest in every county along rivers and lake shores. The
large, bulky nests sit atop tall tree stumps, utility poles, and
nest platforms erected especially for them. Everett hosts a large
nesting population at the Snohomish River mouth. Ospreys
frequently give loud *chirp, chirp, chirp* calls.

Long, narrow, heavily marked wings with big black
wrist patch. Wings held crooked down at wrists.
Brown above, white below, with black stripe through
eye. Head small for raptor, claws very well
developed. Brown speckles on breast usually
indicate female.

Golden Eagle

Aquila chrysaetos

L 30" | **WS** 79"

Golden Eagles are birds of mountains and desert, hunting medium-sized mammals in open country and usually building their bulky nest on a cliff ledge. They are also quite willing to feed on carrion, and are sometimes flushed from the roadside as they dine on roadkill. They occur widely in the Columbia Basin, around the Blue Mountains, and in some of the higher mountain ranges. They can be fairly common locally, but they have large territories, and the best way to see them is to know where they are nesting. They also migrate along Cascade ridges in fall. Golden Eagles soar with wings tilted slightly up, less so than vultures but more so than Bald Eagles. Calls are a series of loud low- to high-pitched chirps.

Large soaring raptor with golden-washed head, well-defined white tail base. Barring in flight feathers not shown by any plumage of Bald. Immature lacks gold on head, has large white primary patches.

Northern Harrier

Circus hudsonius

L 18" | **WS** 43"

Harriers are birds of open countryside, common as wintering birds east and locally common west. The Samish Flats are famous for the number of wintering harriers, more in years when there is a high population of voles. The low, rocking flight with wings held up is characteristic, as are the somewhat owl-like facial disks, testimony to the importance of sound in hunting small prey. They breed locally in wet prairies, and are not uncommon in the Columbia Basin and northward; west of the Cascades, the number of breeders continues to decline. Small numbers migrate along the Cascades with other raptors. Not often heard, they give a rapid series of shrill notes when disturbed at the nest and in aggressive interactions.

Hawk with long tail and prominent white rump patch. Wings held up at substantial angle during gliding, rocking flight. Juvenile (above) has bright buffy underparts.

Facial disks evident at close range. Adult male (left) gray above and white below, gull-like in flight except for the white uppertail coverts. Female brown above, white below with heavy streaks.

Northern Goshawk

Accipiter gentilis

L 21" | **WS** 41"

This is by far the rarest of Washington's three accipiters, or bird hawks, nesting in extensive conifer tracts in the mountain wilderness and in winter wandering out to other habitats, including more open areas. A few are seen in fall migration along mountain ridges. The highest breeding densities are in the Northeastern Highlands. They are very shy at their nests, where a long series of *ki-ki-ki* calls, higher pitched than Cooper's, can be heard. Goshawks are impressive hunters, perfectly adapted to power their way through dense forests, even closing one wing in full flight as they pass between tree trunks. Their prey includes grouse and mammals of rabbit size.

Adult gray above, finely barred gray below, with prominent white eyebrow.

Immature brown above, streaked below, eyebrow not quite as prominent as in adult.

Cooper's Hawk

Accipiter cooperii

L 16.5" | **WS** 31"

Cooper's Hawks are common residents of broadleaf and mixed woodland, and are becoming more common all the time, even in city parks and green belts. They have adapted very well to human presence, and are recovering from low numbers during the pesticide era and from a long history of being persecuted as "chicken hawks." In cities, the abundance of prey species of the right size, from robins to jays to pigeons, surely contributes to their success: there are over 50 nesting pairs in Seattle alone. Males are sometimes seen in display flight above the trees, with slow wingbeats and undertail coverts prominently fluffed out. Calls given around the nest are a long, rapid *kek-kek-kek* series.

Medium-sized hawk, female much larger than male. Tail rounded, outer feathers shorter than central. Flap-and-glide flight. Adult gray above with black cap, heavily barred rufous below.

Immature finely streaked below.

Sharp-shinned Hawk

Accipiter striatus

L 11" | **WS** 23"

Sharp-shinned Hawks nest sparingly in conifer forests throughout the state. Many more are seen migrating down Cascade ridges in fall and lurking in wooded areas in winter, including suburban and urban areas where bird feeders attract the small songbirds that are their prey. Small size (but fierce nature), rounded wings, square tail, and flap-and-glide flight are distinguishing features from other small raptors, but note that females, which are larger than males, are not very much smaller than male Cooper's (measurements given for accipiters are for females). If you live in a wooded area and feed birds, keep your eyes out for both Sharp-shinned and Cooper's. This species gives a high-pitched series of *tew* calls, mostly around the nest.

Small or very small hawk with relatively short rounded wings and long tail. Tail square, outer feathers as long as central. Adult gray above, heavily barred rusty below. Five-flaps-and-a glide flight. Vividly banded tail. Male the size of a Merlin, female considerably larger. Immature brown above, heavily barred and streaked below.

Bald Eagle

Haliaeetus leucocephalus

L 31" | **WS** 80"

Bald Eagles are a conservation success story, taken off the Endangered Species List in 2007. Now there are over 800 breeding pairs in the state, and huge stick nests are visible everywhere on the westside. In fact, eagles are almost shockingly abundant, feeding on spawned-out salmon on big rivers and roosting by the hundreds in riverside cottonwoods in winter. The increase has been less rapid east of the Cascades. In some cases, their depredations on nesting colonies of herons, terns, and murres have become cause for concern. Call is a series of weak, high-pitched, descending squeaky notes.

Immatures mostly brown at first, some with much irregular white patterning in tail and underwing coverts; primaries never barred. Four years to maturity; more white on head and tail with increasing age, while bill and eyes become yellow.

White head and tail on large eagle visible at any distance.

Adult. Huge, yellow-billed soaring raptor with white head and tail.

Swainson's Hawk

Buteo swainsoni

L 19" | **WS** 51"

A buteo hawk soaring with uptilted, pointed wings east of
the Cascades will be a Swainson's. Swainson's Hawks are
confirmed inhabitants of open country, hunting over grassland
and shrub steppe, even over farmland with no pesticides and
thus lots of grasshoppers. They nest in small trees and even
on utility poles. They arrive from South America in late April
and nest quickly; as insect-eaters, they must depart no later
than September for the two-month, 8,000-mile trip back to the
pampas for the winter. Call a shrill *keeeeooo*, sweeter than the
similar scream of a Red-tailed.

Light-morph adult has plain dark
brown upperparts, white throat,
and wide dark breast band.

Wings more pointed than other buteo hawks, tilted up in flight. From below, lightly banded gray flight feathers contrast with pale underwing coverts. Rufous-morph adult's underparts largely reddish. There is also an entirely dark morph, with same wing pattern.

Juvenile dark brown above with fine pale barring. Buffy-white below with scattered bars and streaks. Dark malar stripe.

Red-tailed Hawk

Buteo jamaicensis

L 19" | **WS** 49"

Buteos are hawks with broad wings and broad tails that allow them to soar effortlessly. Red-tailed is the bulky buteo that watches you from utility poles along all lowland highways in Washington. Stop your car a pole or two away, and you can get a good look at this very variable species; immatures are tamer than adults. Watch for birds in the sky as the ground heats up and thermals rise to support their broad wings and tail. Many birds come to Washington in winter to augment the breeding population, concentrating in areas where rodents are common, even at the edges of cities, where they perch on light poles in search of rats. Call a loud, harsh, descending scream.

Stocky, very variable hawk. Underpart color varies from white to reddish to almost black. Light-morph adult dark above, including head; bright coppery tail with narrow black subterminal band.

Dark-morph adult typically reddish below, with prominent streaks across belly. Especially dark birds have dark wing linings and pale, heavily barred flight feathers.

Dark head, lighter breast, and marked belly are typical. From below, contrasting dark markings on leading edge of inner wing and across belly characteristic of all but entirely dark birds. Finely barred brownish tail in all immatures.

Rough-legged Hawk
Buteo lagopus

L 21" | **WS** 53"

Rough-legged Hawks come to us from their Arctic breeding grounds, and are found mostly October–April in open country throughout the eastside, often perched on utility poles. They are much more local west, where they hunt primarily in farmland. The lowland flats in Skagit County are well-known winter haunts in the west. Their principal winter food is voles, and the hawk's abundance varies from winter to winter depending on rodent population cycles. A hawk that hovers with beating wings is probably a Rough-legged; Red-tails hang in the wind with still wings.

Feathered legs. Light-morph adult's pale head and mottled breast contrast with black belly. Large black wrist patches.

Unbarred primaries. Tail band well-defined in adult female, obscure in immature. Dark-morph adult darker above and below.

Ferruginous Hawk

Buteo regalis

L 23" | **WS** 56"

Listed as threatened in Washington, there are probably fewer than 20 breeding pairs of this hawk left in the state. It is present March–August in the southern part of the Columbia Basin; historically, Benton and Franklin Counties have hosted the most nesting pairs. Nests are prominently placed on cliff ledges, in trees, or sometimes on powerline towers. The very large gape lets Ferruginous Hawks eat ground squirrels, rabbits, and pocket gophers, all of which have declined as shrub steppe is converted to agriculture. Calls are longer and sweeter than those of Red-tailed or Swainson's, almost plaintive.

Largest buteo. Light-morph adult white below with rusty leggings; mostly rusty above. Tail all pale.

Dark-morph adult's head and body entirely dark, flight feathers and tail whitish.

Barn Owl

Tyto alba

L 16" | **WS** 42"

Barn Owls are resident throughout the lowlands, where
they roost and nest in tree cavities, on bridge girders, and in
abandoned barns and other buildings. Their presence is often
revealed by regurgitated pellets of hair and bones. Away from
the roost, they are most often seen flying up from nighttime
roadsides, their underparts so white that they are sometimes
mistaken for Snowy Owls. They may come out just before dark
to hunt open areas in search of mice and shrews. Because Barn
Owls, unlike other owls, do not appear to vocally defend their
breeding territories, their populations cannot be surveyed by
listening for territorial calls, making it very difficult to assess
their true abundance. A Barn Owl in flight may give a high-
pitched shriek.

Heart-shaped face,
long legs. Male has
mostly white
underparts, female
mostly buffy below.

Flammulated Owl

Psiloscops flammeolus

L 7" | **WS** 16"

These tiny owls are more difficult to see than any other of
Washington's fairly common land birds. Confirmed insect-
eaters, they are present only May–September, restricted to
ponderosa pine forests on the east side of the Cascades and in
the Northeastern Highlands and Blue Mountains. Their hollow
boop calls can be heard on a still night in early summer, but
these elusive little birds stay high in the trees, where they are
hard to distinguish from their perch. They nest in tree cavities
and are very rarely encountered during the day.

Very small owl with brown eyes, hint
of head tufts. Gray, heavily barred
and streaked, with reddish on face.

Western Screech-Owl

Megascops kennicottii

L 8.5" | **WS** 20"

Gray and mottled like tree bark, screech-owls are resident throughout the state in most types of lowland woodland, including suburban tracts; they are absent from the open Columbia Basin and higher mountains. They nest in tree cavities and bird houses, where one member of the pair can sometimes be seen in the opening. Populations have declined recently on the westside, apparently in part because of predation by Barred Owls. The call is an accelerated series of toots, much like a bouncing ball.

Small owl with big yellow eyes; may show small head tufts. Very gray or strongly brown-tinged, with fine black markings all over.

Great Horned Owl

Bubo virginianus

L 22" | **WS** 44"

Great Horned Owls occur throughout the state in every habitat except alpine parkland and dense wet forest; even wooded city parks may support a pair. They often nest in old hawk nests in trees or on cliff ledges. They prefer to hunt in open areas and along forest edges, taking everything from Red-tailed Hawks on their nests to skunks to housecats; they sometimes hunt late in the afternoon, when they may take tree squirrels or Short-eared Owls. Look for their "whitewash" droppings on basalt cliffs of the Columbia Basin to locate possible roost sites and nests. Males give five loud hoots, females eight.

Large and powerful, with yellow eyes, prominent head tufts. 'Coastal birds are darker, and very pale birds from the Arctic sometimes visit in winter.

Snowy Owl

Bubo scandiacus

L 23" | **WS** 52"

Snowy Owls are sporadic winter visitors to Washington, coming down from the Arctic in numbers November–March every three or four years; these invasions may be becoming less regular as the climate warms. Even in non-invasion years a few are usually seen, especially in the northern Columbia Basin. They can be seen on the ground, rocks, fence posts, and even roofs in open areas ranging from beach dunes and Puget Sound river deltas to interior prairies. Inactive during the day, they begin to hunt as dusk approaches, taking rats and voles in the uplands and grebes, ducks, and sandpipers at the coast. Adult males are very rarely seen this far south.

Large, white, round-headed owl of winter. Adult female finely barred dark all over. Mature male may be almost entirely white.

Immature much more heavily marked than adult. At a distance, looks dark with white face.

Northern Pygmy-Owl

Glaucidium gnoma

L 7" | **WS** 12"

Active by day and into the dusk hours, these very small owls hunt small birds and mammals as large as chipmunks. They are resident in conifer forests at all elevations throughout the state, but are most easily found September–October high in the mountains, when young birds are dispersing. Wintering birds are often encountered in the Okanogan area. Listen for the calls, a repeated hollow toot, sometimes given in rapid sequence. Like other small owls, this is a cavity nester, dependent on woodpeckers for its nest sites.

Tiny diurnal owl, round-headed and small-eyed. Rich brown above with white markings, heavily striped below. When threatened, can change shape dramatically to look like a branch.

Burrowing Owl

Athene cunicularia

L 9.5" | **WS** 21"

Burrowing Owls were formerly common visitors March–August in the open sagebrush and grassland of the southern Columbia Basin, but the expansion of agriculture and the use of pesticides to kill their insect prey have driven numbers to a historic low. Now only scattered pairs are found. They usually nest in the burrows of badgers or marmots, where the male is often visible during the day, standing guard while the female incubates. They hunt large insects and rodents at night. Strongly migratory, Burrowing Owls are also suffering from habitat loss in their winter range. The male's frequently repeated call is a sharp *wau wauuuu*.

Small, long-legged owl seen on ground and fence posts. Round head, yellow eyes. Brown and buff-spotted all over

Spotted Owl
Strix occidentalis

L 17.5" | **WS** 40"

This extremely rare species is listed as endangered in Washington, the result in part of the logging of old-growth coniferous forests, where the few surviving birds feed on red-backed voles and flying squirrels; they cannot thrive in second growth. Now, after decades of controversy, some tracts of forest have been preserved, but Spotted Owls are further endangered by the closely related Barred Owl, which is moving into those forests. Larger and more aggressive, Barred Owls displace Spotted Owls and even hybridize with them wherever the two species come in contact. The call is a distinctive four-note *whoo-hoo-hoo-HOOOO*.

Big, brown-eyed, round-headed owl of old-growth conifer forest. Yellow bill. Brown, heavily spotted white all over.

Barred Owl

Strix varia

L 21" | **WS** 42"

First recorded in Washington in 1965, Barred Owls are now statewide residents in forested landscapes, including small urban woodland parks and backyards. Part of their success is their willingness to prey on all kinds of small animals. Their brown eyes make them look less fierce than Great Horned Owls. The classic description of the territorial call cannot be beat: *who cooks for you, who cooks for you all*. Also listen for the screaming and caterwauling of pairs in the spring.

Big, brown-eyed, round-headed owl of every kind of woodland. Prominently outlined facial disks and yellow bill. Spotted above, but underparts barred and heavily striped.

Great Gray Owl

Strix nebulosa

L 27" | **WS** 52"

With their big facial disks and fluffy plumage, Great Gray Owls look huge, but they actually weigh 20 percent less than a Great Horned Owl. They occur in mature conifer forests, usually adjacent to meadows and forest openings where they hunt pocket gophers and voles. They are best known as breeders in Okanogan and Ferry Counties and also nest in the Blue Mountains. Wintering birds have been seen widely around the state, mostly in the northwestern lowlands, and though they are always rare, more show up in some years than in others. The call is an evenly spaced series of deep hoots.

Large, brownish gray, finely patterned owl with yellow eyes and yellow bill. Huge facial disk clearly outlined.

Long-eared Owl

Asio otus

L 15" | **WS** 36"

Look for wintering Long-eared Owls in groves in the Columbia Basin, especially in stands of trees along the Snake and Columbia Rivers. There are a lot of them, but it can take a lot of searching to find one. Once you have located a roost, it's likely to be there the following winter. Small numbers also nest in such woods, in old magpie nests, but they can be more common when vole populations are high. They are much less common west of the Cascades, found primarily in winter. The "ears" of this and other owls are feather tufts, presumably serving to camouflage roosting birds by making them look like tree stumps. The call is a long series of single hoots a few seconds apart.

Medium-sized, yellow-eyed owl with unusually long, close-set head tufts. Rusty face also distinguishes it from much larger Great Horned. Almost always in "skinny" mode, with body feathers compressed to make bird look more branch-like.

Short-eared Owl

Asio flammeus

L 15" | **WS** 38"

Short-eareds are our common open-country owls, widespread residents of the Columbia Basin, where they nest in open grassland, marshes, and abandoned croplands. They have bred locally west, but most there are October–March migrants from farther north. Variable numbers are present in coastal locations such as Dungeness, Ocean Shores, and Nisqually NWR. They are also on the deltas of the Lummi, Samish, and Skagit Rivers, coursing over fields before dusk in search of voles and most common when those short-tailed rodents reach peak numbers. The short, barking calls can be heard when a Northern Harrier tries to rob one of a fresh-caught vole.

Wings relatively long; swooping flight with deep wingbeats. Prominent buffy primary patches above and black wrist patches below.

Medium-sized owl with round head, yellow eyes, and wide, pale facial disk. Pale and finely streaked below. Short head tufts only occasionally evident. Active at dusk, sometimes during day.

Boreal Owl
Aegolius funereus

L 10" | **WS** 21"

Restricted as breeders to high-elevation spruce/fir/lodgepole pine forests, Boreal Owls have been widely detected by voice, mostly in the eastern Cascades, Northeastern Highlands, and Blue Mountains. They are found most often in fall, when the high country is accessible. Only a few have been found in the lowlands on either side in winter. Roosting in dense vegetation, they are very hard to detect in the daytime, and are surely more common than believed. Male territorial song is a rapid series of >10 hollow toots, with a harsh *skiew* call from time to time.

Small, round-headed owl with yellow eyes. Spotted crown. Vivid black outlines facial disks. Rich brown above, heavily streaked below.

Northern Saw-whet Owl

Aegolius acadicus

L 8" | **WS** 17"

Saw-whets are common breeders in forests throughout the state, but they are not often seen. They can be heard in spring, but when the birds stop calling, their habit of roosting in dense foliage hides them effectively. The male's territorial call is a series of musical toots on one pitch that goes on and on, like striking a xylophone repeatedly. Copses of trees in the Columbia Basin, especially dense spruce, have proven to be good places to search in winter, and migrants even show up in backyards and city parks.

Very small, round-headed owl with yellow eyes. Finely streaked crown, prominent white eyebrows; facial disk not outlined with black.

Belted Kingfisher

Megaceryle alcyon

L 13" | **WS** 20"

Kingfishers are widespread residents in the state, occurring anywhere there is water with fish in it and perches from which to scan—originally trees but now often docks and utility wires. They withdraw from eastside creeks and rivers when they freeze. When hunting, they don't always need perches, as they can dive from the air from momentary hovering positions over the water. They are easy to watch feeding, as their dives are shallow and they usually fly to a nearby perch to beat the fish to death and swallow it headfirst. They nest in long burrows they dig in sand and clay banks, often at the edge of the water. Call is a loud, high-pitched and rapid series of notes that can appropriately be called a rattle.

'Female (shown) blue-gray and white with blue band across chest, rufous band below it and rufous sides. Male lacks rufous; juveniles of both sexes with chestnut in breast band.

Lewis's Woodpecker

Melanerpes lewis

L 11" | **WS** 21"

This is a bird of low- to middle-elevation open woodland east of the Cascades. Breeding habitats including ponderosa pine and Garry oak forests and tall cottonwoods along rivers, where trees are large enough to excavate nest holes. Mostly April–September visitors, many winter in Yakima and Klickitat Counties in years with a good acorn crop. Lewis's Woodpeckers are very conspicuous as they sail around in the sky hunting flying insects, looking like small crows with their rounded wings and steady wingbeats. They are our only woodpeckers that don't undulate in flight. They are relatively quiet, but give high-pitched churring calls.

Adult shiny dark green above, dark red face, gray breast, pinkish belly. Juvenile dark above and gray below, lacking bright colors.

Acorn Woodpecker

Melanerpes formicivorus

L 9" | **WS** 17.5"

Sometimes called "clown woodpeckers" for their garish coloration and comical calls, these birds occur in Washington only
as a tiny breeding population near Lyle in Klickitat County.
Wandering birds have turned up widely in the western lowlands
almost to the Canadian border, and on the eastside to Yakima.
As the name suggests, their preferred habitat is oak woodland.
They live in family groups and breed cooperatively, harvesting
acorns and digging pits in dead trees to cache them by the
thousands for winter food. These "granaries" can be a good sign
of their presence. They are noisy, the oft-repeated two-note call
sounding like *jacob jacob jacob jacob.*

Black and white woodpecker
with fancy head pattern and
prominent white eyes.
Conspicuous white wing
patches in flight. Male has
red crown, female black
band separating red and
white.

Williamson's Sapsucker

Sphyrapicus thyroideus

L 9" | **WS** 17"

One of the birds most closely associated with larches, the Williamson's Sapsucker is a common visitor May–September to the east slope of the Cascades in ponderosa pine/western larch forests. It is less common in the Northeastern Highlands and Blue Mountains. The striking difference in appearance between the sexes is unusual in woodpeckers. Call is a repeated harsh *chyahh, chyahh, chyahh,* lower pitched than other sapsuckers. The drumming has a distinct rhythm, in contrast to the irregular drumming of Red-naped Sapsuckers, which often occur in the same habitat.

Male mostly black, with white head stripes and large white wing patch. Small red throat patch, yellow belly.

Female heavily barred black and white, with mostly brown head, black upper breast, and yellow belly.

Red-naped Sapsucker

Sphyrapicus nuchalis

L 8.5" | **WS** 16"

Red-naped Sapsuckers occur April–September in forested areas from the east side of the Cascades east. They prefer broadleaf trees for nesting, and are especially common in riparian corridors dominated by aspens. Their high-pitched squeals and irregular drumming are good signs of their presence, as are the rows of small holes they drill into the bark of their preferred trees. These holes leak the sap that is their primary food, but they also take insects attracted to the sap and feed them to their young. Hummingbirds, songbirds, and even squirrels also come to these "wells" for sap.

Black and white with barred back, long white wing stripe. Male's crown, throat, and small nape patch red. Dull and finely barred below, center of belly unmarked. Female's throat varies from white to mostly red. Juvenile dark and obscurely patterned, but white wing stripe still prominent.

Red-breasted Sapsucker

Sphyrapicus ruber

L 8.5" | **WS** 16"

Red-breasted Sapsuckers are resident throughout the lowlands of western Washington and up to timberline in the Cascades. Small numbers also occur in summer on the eastern slopes of that mountain range, from Okanogan to Yakima County, where they hybridize with Red-naped Sapsuckers. Watch for birds with every sort of intermediate head pattern. During extreme cold periods, when the sap freezes in mountain trees, Red-breasteds descend in large numbers to the western lowlands, appearing far from nest sites. Calls and drumming are similar to those of Red-naped.

Like Red-naped, but head and upper breast mostly red. Juvenile dark and dull, but white wing stripe prominent.

American Three-toed Woodpecker

Picoides dorsalis

L 9" | **WS** 15"

Washington's high-elevation woodpecker, this species occurs from timberline down to about 4,000 feet in all the state's mountain ranges—Olympics, Cascades, Northeastern Highlands, and Blue Mountains—but it is not common and is often hard to find. It is most common in stands of Engelmann spruce, especially burned forests; look for scaled-off bark as an indication of the presence of this species and Black-backed. White back varies from heavily to sparsely barred with black, but barred sides distinguish white-backed birds from Hairy Woodpecker. The call is a sharp *pik*. This and Black-backed are our only three-toed woodpeckers.

Black and white with heavily barred back, barred sides, and white head stripes. Yellow crown only in male.

Black-backed Woodpecker

Picoides arcticus

L 9.5" | **WS** 16"

The Black-backed Woodpecker is an eastside species, from the Cascade crest east. Unlike the American Three-toed, its range also extends down into the ponderosa pine zone. This is a firebird, appearing at extensive recent burns; Black-backed Woodpeckers compete with American Three-toed and Hairy Woodpeckers for the beetle larvae in the dead and dying trees. The beetles decline after a few years, and the woodpeckers move on. The call is a rapid clicking, softer than that of the other black-and-white forest woodpeckers.

Shiny black head and back, only one white head stripe. White underparts with sparsely barred sides. Yellow crown only in male.

Downy Woodpecker
Dryobates pubescens

L 7" | **WS** 12"

Diminutive Downy Woodpeckers are widespread residents, preferring broadleaf trees and shrubs and occurring just about everywhere in the lowlands, including along all the streams and rivers in the Columbia Basin and well-wooded suburbs state-wide. You may even see one foraging on a tall mullein stalk in a field. Most juvenile woodpeckers can be distinguished by sex; juvenile male Downies have a red crown, not the red patch on the nape that distinguishes adults. Juvenile females rarely have a few red crown feathers. Calls are a soft *pik* and a "whinny" of rapid *pik* notes descending at the end. Drumming is steady and all on one pitch.

Male. Black and white woodpecker with white stripe down back, petite bill. Black spots in outer tail feathers. Coastal birds tinged with brown on head and underparts.

Female. Lacks red on head. Interior birds white below.

Hairy Woodpecker

Dryobates villosus

L 9" | **WS** 15"

More than twice the weight of the very similar Downy, this is the woodpecker of conifers, resident everywhere in pine and fir and spruce forests throughout the state and up to tree line. They may forego conifers locally, especially in the suburbs, where they may even be seen with Downies at feeders. Hairies are also common at burns along with Black-backed Woodpeckers, and their plumage may get very worn at such times. Juvenile plumages are like those of Downy. Calls are a loud *pik*, much more forceful than Downy, and a rapid series of the same notes remaining at the same level. Drumming is more rapid than that of Downy, with longer pauses between bursts.

Male. Black and white woodpecker with white stripe down back, bill impressive. Interior subspecies white below.

Female. Lacks red on head. Coastal subspecies brownish tinged on head and underparts.

White-headed Woodpecker

Dryobates albolarvatus

L 9" | **WS** 16"

These well-named birds are resident, virtually confined to ponderosa pine forests on the east slope of the Cascades, North-eastern Highlands, and Blue Mountains. They are most common in southern Kittitas and Yakima counties. They scale bark off the trees and remove seeds from cones while foraging, behavior different from that of the Hairy Woodpeckers that are also common in the same habitat. The calls include a shrill double note *pee-dik* and a rattled call much like the Hairy's.

Black woodpecker with white head, big white wing patch. Male with red on back of head.

Northern Flicker

Colaptes auratus

L 12.5" | **WS** 20"

These are our most common and widespread woodpeckers, unusual in being almost entirely ground foragers—thus, the brown camouflage—and very commonly feeding on ants. They can be seen in open country in winter but need trees for nesting. They take well to humans and are common in well-wooded cities, coming to feeders of all kinds. Fruiting trees also attract them in winter. Yellow-shafted flickers from farther north interbreed with our red-shafted ones where they meet, producing intermediate-looking hybrids that are not uncommon in Washington; pure yellow-shafted also visit during winter. Flickers give a *wicka wicka wicka* call frequently, and the territorial call is a long series *wik-wik-wik* etc.

Heavily barred with black above and spotted with black below. Black crescent across breast. In red-shafted birds, wing and tail feathers reddish below; no red on nape. Female lacks red facial stripe.

In more northerly, yellow-shafted birds, wing and tail feathers yellow below; red patch on nape. Female lacks black facial stripe.

Pileated Woodpecker

Dryocopus pileatus

L 16.5" | **WS** 29"

These woodpecker giants are resident in forests throughout the state, wherever the trees are large enough for their big nest cavities. Increasingly tolerant of humans, they are now found in parks and wooded areas in most of our large cities, where they readily visit suet feeders, to the delight of all who see them. Their presence is revealed by the deep oval-shaped gouges they excavate in dead trees in search of long-horned beetle and carpenter ant larvae. The long call is louder, richer, and more hollow sounding than that of flickers, and their drumming is louder and more resonant than that of any other woodpecker.

Huge, mostly black, red-crested woodpecker. Male's striped head pattern includes red crown and red facial stripe. Eyes pale yellow. Front of crown and facial stripe black in female. Eyes slightly darker.

American Kestrel

Falco sparverius

L 9-12" | **WS** 20-24"

Kestrels are widespread in Washington in open and semiopen country, especially in the Columbia Basin, where they can be seen perched along the utility wires. Much more local as breeders west, their numbers increase with the arrival of wintering birds, but they are still much less common there than they are east. They withdraw from higher elevations in the winter. They nest in tree holes and cliff crevices, and readily accept nest boxes. They feed primarily on insects and lizards in summer, small mammals in winter. The call is a loud, shrill *kilee kilee kilee kilee kilee*.

Small falcon with pointed wings, rusty back and tail. Face with two vertical dark stripes. Male (left) with blue-gray wings and wide band on tail. Female (below) entirely rusty above with narrow tail bands.

Merlin
Falco columbarius

L 10" | **WS** 24"

These small, lightning-fast falcons are often seen hot on the tail of smaller birds, from sandpipers to juncos. They migrate and winter throughout the state in forested and open habitats. Breeding is more and more frequent in the lowlands, often in urban situations where there is an abundance of small birds; these birds even take hummingbirds. Merlins lay their four eggs in disused crow nests. Wintering and migrant individuals are usually seen out in the open hunting Dunlins and other shorebirds. They only rarely perch on the utility wires that kestrels prefer. The most common call is a series of *kee-kee-kee-kee* notes at varying speeds.

Small falcon with dashing flight. Migrant male with gray upperparts, prominent eyebrow, heavily streaked underparts, white-barred tail.

Resident breeders, "Black Merlins," are blackish and more heavily streaked, without pale eyebrow; may lack tail markings. Dragonflies are frequent in the diet.

Peregrine Falcon

Falco peregrinus

L 16" | **WS** 41"

It is gratifying to see the dramatic recovery of these apex avian predators after their brush with extinction in the DDT era. Their level flight is swift and direct, and they dive at dazzling speeds after avian prey; baffles in the nostrils keep the wind out. Bonaparte's Gulls, Green-winged Teals, and flickers are among the favored prey, but Peregrines take birds ranging in size from sandpipers to geese. They nest on cliffs in the San Juan Islands and on buildings and bridges in Seattle. Many more pass through the state in migration and spend the winter, especially along the coast. Call is a loud *cack cack cack cack,* heard mostly from pairs around the nest.

Large falcon. Gray above, with darker head and broad black facial stripe. Peach-colored below, with barred flanks; male paler below than female shown here. Migrant Peregrines from the Arctic paler, with patterned head and narrow facial stripe. Breeding birds more black and white. Powerful flight on long, pointed wings. Immature (left) brown above, heavily streaked below. Narrow pale eyebrow and black facial streak. Wing and tail feathers heavily barred.

Prairie Falcon

Falco mexicanus

L 16" | **WS** 40"

Prairie Falcons are residents of open country in the Columbia Basin. Many migrate out of the state in fall, some of them moving upslope to high elevations on the east side of the Cascades. They are rare in winter in western Washington, most often seen in the Skagit County lowlands. They take a wide variety of prey, including ground squirrels, meadowlarks, doves, and larks. No falcons build their own nest, but Prairie Falcons do scrape debris together into a small depression to hold their eggs, usually on high cliff ledges. Mated pairs give *cack* calls similar to those of Peregrines, especially directed at intruders near a nest.

Peregrine-sized, but sandy brown all over. Narrow dark facial stripe. Tail obscurely patterned.

Dark axilars and wing linings obvious in flight. Sides may also be heavily patterned with black.

Ash-throated Flycatcher

Myiarchus cinerascens

L 8.5" | **WS** 12"

Ash-throated Flycatchers are visitors May–August to oak and riparian woodland in Yakima, Klickitat, and southern Kittitas Counties, with scattered birds farther north and east. They forage mostly at low levels, moving from perch to perch and flying out to capture adult and larval insects detected on the ground or vegetation. This is our only flycatcher that nests in natural or artificial cavities. Variable calls include high-pitched *brit*, *chi-brit*, and *ch-ch-beer*.

Large, long-tailed flycatcher with puffy crest, gray breast, pale yellow belly, and rusty feathers in wings and tail.

Western Kingbird

Tyrannus verticalis

L 9" ｜ **WS** 15.5"

Western Kingbirds are present from late April through August throughout the Columbia Basin and other open areas in the eastside lowlands. A few pairs nest in similar habitats west of the Cascades, for example in Fort Lewis and along the Skagit River. Migrants turn up on the westside fairly frequently in spring, rarely in fall. The best place to look for them is on utility wires, which they use as hunting perches. They use utility poles as nest sites, with prominent nests often placed between a transformer and the pole. As is typical of all kingbirds, they persistently harass hawks and other larger birds. Calls include a sharp *pi-dick* and longer variations.

Upright perching typical of most flycatchers. Large flycatcher with yellow belly and gray head, back, and breast. Black tail with white outer edges. Concealed red and yellow feathers in center of crown occasionally displayed.

Eastern Kingbird

Tyrannus tyrannus

L 8.5" | **WS** 15"

Eastern Kingbirds are common visitors mid–May to August throughout the open landscapes of eastern Washington, with occasional breeding west along the Snohomish River and from Rockport to Marblemount. They are likely to be seen on utility wires, but are much more restricted to sites near water than Westerns. Mature willows around any pond or stream are likely to have a pair. The bright red to yellow crown is hidden except during some displays; it is lacking in juveniles, which otherwise resemble adults. Calls are a loud *dzeeb* and *dzibba-dzibba-dzeeb*, more strident when a crow or raven or hawk is detected, at which time both members of the pair dive at it unmercifully, even riding on the larger bird's back to get in a few pecks.

Slightly smaller than Western Kingbird. Black and white with white tail tip.

Olive-sided Flycatcher

Contopus cooperi

L 7.5" | **WS** 13"

Olive-sided Flycatchers are summer visitors, common May to early September throughout our conifer forests. They forage from the highest branches of tall trees, sallying high into the air after insects, and thus are more easily seen at forest edges, such as along lakeshores or even in clearcuts. Migrants are occasionally seen in open country. The loud, whistled *quick THREE BEERS* of the Olive-sided is one of the most striking flycatcher songs. They also frequently give *pip pip pip* calls.

Smaller than kingbirds, with long wings and relatively short tail. Perches upright. Olive-brown back. "Unbuttoned vest," white streak down underparts bordered by gray streaks on breast sides. Often erects short crest.

Western Wood-Pewee

Contopus sordidulus

L 6" | **WS** 10.5"

Western Wood-Pewees are common visitors May–September in dry conifer forests and riparian woodland east, much less common in wetter forests west. They are absent as breeding birds from most of the Columbia Basin, but are regularly seen there in spring and fall migration. Unlike the larger and Olive-sided Flycatcher, they are not found very high in the mountains. The primary song is a raspy, downward-inflected *beeurr*. Singing persists throughout the day and throughout the summer, longer than in most birds.

Smaller than Olive-sided, with relatively longer tail, less robust bill, and less conspicuous vest. Lacks eye ring typical of most Empidonax flycatchers, which are noticeably smaller than pewees and have distinctive tail motions.

Willow Flycatcher

Empidonax traillii

L 6" | **WS** 8.5"

There are five small flycatchers in Washington in the genus *Empidonax*. They are considered among the most challenging of North American birds to identify in the field, but learning their nesting habitats, songs, and calls will aid in identification. All five differ from wood-pewees in their smaller size, shorter wings, and usually conspicuous eye rings. The Willow breeds in riparian strips, willow thickets, and regenerating clearcuts in forested parts of the state. A late spring migrant from northern South America, it is present from the end of May to mid-September. The song is a spirited *sneezy FITZ-bew*, and the common call is a light *whit*.

Only *Empidonax* flycatcher without conspicuous eye ring. Quite brownish above, with whitish breast and some pale yellow on belly. Broad-based lower mandible yellow. Shorter wing, smaller size, and tail-flicking distinguish it from pewees.

Hammond's Flycatcher

Empidonax hammondii

L 5.5" | **WS** 9"

Hammond's Flycatcher is the Empidonax of the upper story of conifer and mixed forests throughout the state, common May–September. It is often seen in migration in other habitats. As they complete their annual molt while still on the breeding grounds, Hammond's stay in Washington later than Dusky and Gray Flycatchers, which live in drier, less productive habitats and thus migrate to their wintering grounds before they molt. The song is two or three sets of doubled notes, the first set accented on the first syllable: *SEEdick prrit pewit*. Call is a sharp *peek*, perhaps the surest clue to identification.

Greenish gray, with relatively dark breast, pale belly with some yellowish tinge. Bill quite small and dark, only slight hint of yellow at base of lower mandible. Wings long for an *Empidonax*, reaching well down length of tail. Much smaller than pewees; flicks tail and often wings.

Gray Flycatcher

Empidonax wrightii

L 6" | **WS** 9"

Gray Flycatchers are locally common visitors May–August in open ponderosa pine forests from Klickitat to Okanogan and east to Spokane County. They are easily distinguished from other *Empidonax* flycatchers by their habit of sedately dipping the tail down and then up again. The Dusky and other *Empidonax* species flick the tail upward. The song is a two-syllabled *chedip*, often repeated, and at times accompanied by *cheep*. Call is a *whit* like that of Willow or Dusky.

Rather drab and colorless looking. Bill relatively long and narrow, with much yellow on lower mandible. Plumage most similar to Dusky, but note different tail motion, a leisurely downward wag rather than a sharp upward flick.

Dusky Flycatcher

Empidonax oberholseri

L 6" | **WS** 8"

Dusky Flycatchers are common visitors May–August in
conifer forests from the Cascades east. On the eastside, they
are frequently in the same general area as Hammond's, but
invariably prefer more open forests, where they forage in the
understory, even in shrub thickets; Hammond's Flycatchers
are more likely to feed high in the canopy. The Dusky's song
comprises three sets of two notes, *seDICK prrit peeWEET,*
the first set accented on the second syllable. They also sing a
mournful *doohic.* Call is a *whit* resembling that of the Willow
Flycatcher, quite different from the sharp, explosive *peek* of
the Hammond's.

Brownish gray upperparts
and breast, paler belly
often with some yellowish.
Bill fairly long, yellow at
base of lower mandible.
Wings fall short of end of
undertail coverts.

Pacific-slope Flycatcher

Empidonax difficilis

L 5.5" | **WS** 8"

Pacific-slope Flycatchers breed all across the state in dense, wet forests with open understory and in some riparian woodlands. They are the common *Empidonax* throughout the Olympic Peninsula from May to early September, and are regularly seen as migrants elsewhere. They forage for insects in the dense, dimly lit foliage under the forest canopy. The male's high-pitched and upward-inflected *pseeet* call is distinctive, and the song elaborates on it: *pi-dick seet piseet*.

Yellowest *Empidonax*, with much yellow on underparts. Wide bill with yellow lower mandible. Eye ring teardrop-shaped, extending back from eye.

Say's Phoebe

Sayornis saya

L 7.5" | **WS** 13"

Say's Phoebes are birds of open country throughout the Columbia Basin and in similar habitats elsewhere on the east-side. Arriving as early as late February, they look for nest sites on cliff ledges or on buildings, abandoned or not. Look for them around farms and houses in the country, where their vigorous downward tail dipping attracts attention. They nest every year at the Ginkgo Petrified Forest State Park Interpretive Center. More than our other flycatchers, they feed on ground-dwelling insects. Eastside breeders are gone by the end of September, but migrants linger later on the westside, where they are also frequently seen March–May. Call is a plaintive *peeur*.

Medium-sized flycatcher with slight crest. Drab brownish with darker cap, salmon-colored belly. All-black tail distinctive in flight.

Loggerhead Shrike

Lanius ludovicianus

L 9" | **WS** 12"

With their black "bandit" masks, shrikes are our only small
birds that regularly prey on vertebrates. Loggerheads supplement their insect diet with lizards and occasional small birds
and mammals. They are found in the Columbia Basin from late
March to mid–August, but when the insects disappear for the
winter, so do most of Washington's Loggerhead Shrikes. A few
winter at the lowest elevations. Their calls are low-pitched and
harsh, but the song is a long, slow series of soft, well-spaced
whistled notes.

Hooked bill. Gray and white, with
broad black mask and black-and-
white wings and tail.

Northern Shrike

Lanius borealis

L 10" | **WS** 14.5"

Arriving after most Loggerheads have departed, the slightly larger Northern Shrike is a statewide visitor October–March in lower-elevation open country, including large clearings in forested landscapes. Northern Shrikes feed on voles and sparrow-sized songbirds, and like their smaller relative skewer prey on thorns and barbed-wire fences to eat a bit and return to later. The song is a complex mix of harsh and musical notes, sometimes heard from wintering birds before they depart. They occasionally give harsh alarm calls.

Adult paler than Loggerhead, with narrower mask. Finely barred below. Immature brown, with strongly barred underparts and bill pale at base

Hutton's Vireo

Vireo huttoni

L 5" | **WS** 8"

Hutton's Vireo is a widespread resident of forests with a large component of broadleaf trees through the western lowlands and up the Columbia River to Skamania County. This is our smallest vireo, not much larger than the very similar Ruby-crowned Kinglet, with which it often associates in winter. Unlike the kinglet, the vireo's broken eye ring connects with the vaguely paler lore; its bill is also thicker, as are its gray feet, and the wing lacks the blackish patch between the wingbars that identifies the kinglet. The song, given from February into April, is a monotonously repeated *shiree shiree shiree*, with harsh chattering as an alarm call.

Vireos are woodland birds whose prominent bills are heavier than those of warblers but not flat like those of flycatchers. The Hutton's is small, with wingbars and eye rings.

Cassin's Vireo

Vireo cassinii

L 5.5" | **WS** 9.5"

Cassin's Vireos are visitors mid–April to mid–September
in drier conifer forests dominated by ponderosa pine and
Douglas-fir, where they feed well up in the tree canopy. They
are distributed through the Puget Trough, Cascades, Northeastern Highlands, and Blue Mountains up to moderate
elevations, but are absent from the wet outer coast. The song
is a series of 2- or 3-note musical phrases repeated again and
again, with a burry element absent from the Red-eyed Vireo's
song; the call is a harsh chatter.

Prominent white spectacles and
wingbars. Gray head contrasts
with more greenish back and sides
and white throat.

Warbling Vireo

Vireo gilvus

L 5.5" | **WS** 8.5"

Warbling Vireos are surely among the dullest of birds in Washington, but they are common and widespread and, like all other birds, worthy of a second look. They breed in all wooded parts of the state up into the subalpine zone, preferring woodlands with a large component of deciduous trees. They are present from May to mid-September and are among the more common migrants throughout the state. They tend to forage lower than the other two migratory vireos. The song is complex, with an up-and-down beat. It starts and stops, unlike the continuous songs of the other vireos.

Whitish eyebrow and lack of wingbars are distinctive.

Red-eyed Vireo

Vireo olivaceus

L 6" | **WS** 10"

Red-eyed Vireos do not appear in Washington until mid–May or even later, and all head back to South America by mid–September. They are best found in tall riparian cottonwoods, most commonly in the major river valleys of the northeast, but they also occur on the westside in mature deciduous forests dominated by bigleaf maples. They usually stay high in the canopy, where they are most easily located by their song, a series of musical multi-noted phrases that can go on and on, even through a hot summer afternoon. The call is a chatter.

Like Warbling with white eyebrows and no wingbars, but larger, greener above, and whiter below. Dark eye line and border to gray crown create stronger head pattern. Red eyes visible only at close range.

Canada Jay
Perisoreus canadensis

L 11.5" | **WS** 18"

Canada Jays are widespread in all of Washington's mountain ranges up to the subalpine, especially in denser forests above 3,000 feet. Though mostly absent from the Puget Trough, they are seen at Lewis and Clark SP and other scattered sites. They are also locally common on the Olympic Peninsula and in southwestern lowlands out to the coast. Smart and curious birds, they have learned to approach hikers and backpackers anywhere for a snack. They travel in family groups throughout the year, and can be located by their great variety of musical and harsh notes, including descending *wheeoo* whistles. Birds in the Northeastern Highlands and Blue Mountains have less black on the head than those in the Cascades and west.

Short bill. Gray to gray-brown above and whitish to dull gray below, with variable black markings on head. Juvenile very different from adult, entirely medium to dark gray, with vague whitish streak on face. Almost always seen in flocks with adults.

Clark's Nutcracker

Nucifraga columbiana

L 12" | **WS** 24"

Nutcrackers are pine-seed specialists. More common in the Cascades than in the Olympics, they occur mostly in the subalpine zone, where whitebark pine is common . They store up to 150 pine seeds, equivalent to up to 20 percent of their weight, in a special pouch under the tongue, and travel up to 5 miles to cache the seeds in the ground or in bark crevices for the winter. When whitebark undergoes a coneless year, high-mountain birds move downslope east of the Cascades to harvest ponderosa seeds. They also breed in ponderosa pine forests. They shamelessly beg for food at high-elevation parking lots on Mount Rainier and at ski resorts. They are often seen in flight overhead, giving their grating *kraaak* calls.

Long-billed and short-tailed, shaped more like a crow than a jay. Gray; black wings and tail with white patches.

California Scrub-Jay

Aphelocoma californica

L 11.5" | **WS** 15.5"

Restricted mostly to Clark and Klickitat Counties 50 years ago, scrub-jays are now widespread but local in much of the lowlands of western Washington; they are rare on the Olympic Peninsula and absent from the larger islands of the Puget Trough. They are also widespread in Klickitat and Yakima Counties, and have moved up the Columbia River to the Tri-Cities. Originally oak-woodland birds, with acorns their major food, they are comfortable around people, and like Steller's Jays, now readily visit feeders where suburbs have opened up the dense forests. Call is a loud *zhreek*.

Blue, gray, and white, with long tail and no crest. Contrasting head pattern, faint white eyebrow. Juvenile has mostly brown head, little hint of eyebrow.

Steller's Jay

Cyanocitta stelleri

L 11.5" | **WS** 19"

Steller's Jays are widespread in all forested parts of the state, from high in the mountain ranges to the lower edge of ponderosa pine and oak woodland east, and throughout the lowlands west. Adaptable and familiar in towns and cities, they ransack feeders and quickly learn to peck at a window to get a peanut tossed to them. Common calls are a repeated *shook shook shook*; listen for the male's song of gurgles and whistles, and watch the expressive crest when two birds interact. Jays and crows and their relatives are "corvids," members of the family Corvidae. Universally smart and adaptable, they are among our most successful birds.

Black and blue, with long, expressive crest. Juvenile lacks blue forehead markings.

Common Raven

Corvus corax

L 22–24" | **WS** 44–47"

Present throughout Washington, ravens are birds of open landscapes as varied as the Columbia Basin and subalpine mountaintops. They are least common in the Puget Trough, where they are slowly increasing, much to the consternation of the local crows. As potential predators of eggs and young birds, ravens flying over crow territories are invariably chased away. Their predatory habits are also implicated in the decline of Washington's sage-grouse. Ravens are the largest songbirds in the world, and along with their familiar ringing croaks, they make many other sounds, some of them quite musical. They soar much more than crows, and tend not to flock except at dumps, such as those at Ephrata and Yakima.

Twice the size of a crow, with relatively larger bill, longer tail. Scruffy and browner in September. Throat feathers slender and pointed in adult, juvenile with normal throat feathers. Wings relatively longer than in crows; tail longer, somewhat wedge-shaped, with longer central feathers. Large bill.

American Crow

Corvus brachyrhynchos

L 17" | **WS** 36"

Crows are birds of open woodland rather than dense forest, so as our forests have been cleared and countless trees planted in open areas, they have colonized much of the state. They are still scarce at high elevations, in treeless areas of the Columbia Basin, and in extensively forested areas such as the interior of the Olympic Peninsula. Thousands gather in spectacular fashion on late winter afternoons to roost at locations such as the University of Washington campus in Bothell. The crow's *caw* is familiar to all, but the calls of ours are a bit flatter, not as musical as those in most of the country.

Shiny black. Just before September molt, brownish and distinctly scruffier. Juvenile duller, no iridescence; young juveniles with blue eyes.

All black. Tail square-tipped, rounded when spread. Sometimes in large flocks.

Black-billed Magpie

Pica hudsonia

L 19" | **WS** 25"

Magpies, with their flashy colors and long tail, are resident in open country in the lowlands of the Columbia Basin and the major river valleys east. A cluster of Seattle records may be of released cagebirds. Magpies are omnivores, taking carrion, small mammals, seeds, and fruit with equal enthusiasm. Their spherical nests are conspicuous in the spring in leafless trees; sometimes a Long-eared Owl pair will take up residence in last year's magpie nest. In winter, dozens of magpies may gather at local roosts. Calls are a high-pitched *meeah* and a rapid musical chattering.

Long-tailed black and white bird of open country. Big white wing patches flash in flight. Juvenile less iridescent than adult, with shorter tail.

Horned Lark

Eremophila alpestris

L 7" | **WS** 12"

Horned Larks are birds of wide-open spaces, with three distinct populations breeding in Washington. The endangered Streaked Horned Lark is restricted to the Tacoma Prairies, several airports, and the south coast. Other, much larger populations breed in the alpine zone of the Cascades and Olympics and throughout the shrub steppe and wheat fields of the Columbia Basin. Migrants, including larks breeding in the Arctic, occur all across the state; the Columbia Basin hosts large wintering flocks. This species breeds very early, and males begin to sing their lovely tinkling song from the ground and in the air in February. Horned Larks differ from other open-country birds by their black, white-edged tails, visible as they fly overhead.

Dark tail with white edges. Reddish-sandy ground feeder with vivid head markings, including black, horn-like feather tufts in male. Female with duller face pattern, smaller and less conspicuous "horns."

Violet-green Swallow

Tachycineta thalassina

L 5" | **WS** 13.5"

Violet-green Swallows occur throughout the state from late
February to September, high in the mountains and across the
Columbia Basin alike. Originally nesting in cliff crevices and
tree cavities, they are now common urban birds, breeding in
nest boxes and cavities of all kinds in buildings, light fixtures,
and signs. At the beginning of fall migration, Violet-greens
and other swallows gather in large numbers on utility wires at
staging areas. The song and calls are a series of rapid twittering
notes interspersed with more complex phrases.

Tail shallowly forked. Male metallic green above with
violet rump; white below, white of face extending behind
eye. Conspicuous white rump patches in both sexes. Flight
with much fluttering, while Tree Swallows glide more.
Female brownish, but iridescence visible in good light.

Tree Swallow

Tachycineta bicolor

L 6" | **WS** 14.5"

Among the earliest birds to return from the south, Tree Swallows arrive in Washington in late February; they depart in August. They occur throughout the state, but are absent from the highest mountains and from large parts of the Columbia Basin where there are no suitable bodies of water. They prefer to nest over or near water in tree cavities, and they also breed in nest boxes, especially boxes on poles in the water. First-year females and juveniles are brown above. Calls are a diverse mix of chirps, gurgles, and chatters, given at the nest or in flight.

Adults of both sexes metallic dark green or blue-green above, white below, with sharp transition. Tail shallowly forked. Female similar to juvenile in first year.

Bank Swallow

Riparia riparia

L 5" | **WS** 13"

Present in Washington late April to September, Bank Swallows breed in colonies larger than those of any other swallow. On the westside, colonies tend to be smaller; there are more colonies east, some of them very large, for example, the estimated 5,000 pairs at White Bluffs on the Columbia River. They nest in two-foot-long burrows in sand banks along rivers, road cuts, and even sand piles for construction projects. Colonies must relocate when their nesting banks collapse. The male of a pair follows the female when she leaves the nest to keep neighboring males from trying to mate with her. Calls are short, harsh buzzes, like the crackling of utility wires; colonies are very noisy.

Smallest swallow. Brown above, white below, with obvious brown breast band. Back paler than wing and tail feathers. Rapid, powerful wing beats quite different from slow, deliberate flight of Northern Rough-winged.

Northern Rough-winged Swallow

Stelgidopteryx serripennis

L 5.5" | **WS** 14"

These brown swallows with their characteristic slow, batlike flight are present in the lowlands of Washington from mid-March into September. They occur throughout the state where there are banks for nesting, but in smaller numbers than the other swallows. Look for these and other swallows capturing insects over water bodies on cool days in early spring. Rough-wings do not dig their own burrows, but build their nests in cavities of all sorts, from abandoned Bank Swallow holes to pipes protruding from banks. Calls are short *churring* sounds.

Mostly brown, including throat and upper breast; white from lower breast to undertail coverts. Tiny bill and feet like those of other swallows.

Cliff Swallow

Petrochelidon pyrrhonota

L 5.5" | **WS** 13.5"

Present from late March to September, Cliff Swallows nest all across the lowlands of the state in colonies of up to a few hundred. They still nest on cliffs throughout the coulees of the Columbia Basin, but they have also learned to nest under bridges and on barns and other human structures. To build their gourd-shaped nests, they collect mud from a nearby pond or puddle in their bill, flying to and from the colony one load at a time to plaster it onto the wall; the entire process requires about 24 hours. They give high-pitched, sometimes squeaky *cheer* calls, deafening in a colony.

Metallic blue above, with pale stripes on back. Forehead cream, throat dark chestnut. Dark throat and square tail obvious from below in flight, buff rump patch from above. Often seen on ground gathering mud. Juvenile with darker forehead and often pale throat.

Barn Swallow

Hirundo rustica

L 7" | **WS** 15"

Barn Swallows are present April–September throughout the state's lowlands. They originally placed their open mud nests on cliff ledges, but have almost completely abandoned natural sites for ledges under bridges and under the eaves of houses and other buildings. Using such real estate probably keeps nests safer from predators and rain, but it doesn't always endear the swallows to homeowners. The swallows range far and wide from the nest, foraging low over meadows. Call a clipped *vik* or *k-vik*.

Often flies lower than other swallows. Graceful, with long, deeply forked tail. Dark metallic blue above, orange below, with darker throat. Male's tail fork longer than female's.

In all plumages, conspicous white bar across spread tail. Juvenile paler below than adult, tail shorter.

Purple Martin

Progne subis

L 8" | **WS** 18"

These large, dark swallows are summer visitors, present in
Washington from mid-April to mid-September. They have
declined greatly, in part because starlings take over their nest
cavities, but great efforts are being made to increase their
Washington populations by putting out nest boxes on pilings.
These efforts have been fairly successful, and at present those
boxes may house the only martin nests in some parts of the
state. There are now many nesting pairs scattered throughout
the western Washington lowlands and up the Columbia River to
Klickitat County. The calls are loud liquid whistles, some with
a burry quality.

Largest swallow, with
prominently forked tail.
Often fly so high that
they are detected only
by their calls. Male all
shiny blue-black.

Female's upperparts
metallic, underparts
white to speckled
brown; throat usually
darker. Gray band on
hindneck. First-year
male similar, but
usually with some
blue-black feathers on
head and breast.

Black-capped Chickadee

Poecile atricapillus

L 5" | **WS** 8"

Black-capped Chickadees are common inhabitants of lowland deciduous growth throughout the state, including both unbroken forests and riparian strips. They are absent from the higher mountains, scarce in most of the Columbia Basin, generally uncommon on the Olympic Peninsula, and largely absent from the San Juan Islands. They are well adapted to suburbia, visiting feeders and nesting in nest boxes and in cavities they excavate themselves. The *chickadee-dee-dee* call is well known. In spring, males whistle *SEE-deee* or *SEE-dee-dee*; westside birds often sing four notes.

Chickadees are small, active birds with moderate-length tails, dark cap and throat, and white cheeks. Head markings in this species black. Gray upperparts and buffy sides on westside; paler below, with slightly longer tail, on eastside.

Mountain Chickadee

Poecile gambeli

L 5" | **WS** 8.5"

Mountain Chickadees occur throughout the east side of the Cascades, the Northeastern Highlands, and the Blue Mountains, from the lower edge of the ponderosa pine forest to timberline. They often occur with Black-capped where moist streamside vegetation grades into conifer stands, and they are equally at home in some of the suburbs of eastern Washington, especially those with pines, such as around Spokane. The longer, thinner bill is an adaptation for probing clusters of conifer needles. The buzzy chickadee calls sound like a Black-capped with a cold; spring whistles are *SEEE-dee-dee*.

Pale and long-tailed, with white eyebrow and more extensive white cheeks than Black-capped. Sides grayer.

Chestnut-backed Chickadee

Poecile rufescens

L 5" | **WS** 7.5"

The Chestnut-backed is the chickadee of wet conifer forests from the upper slopes of the Cascades west to the coast and of higher-elevation forests in the Northeastern Highlands and Blue Mountains. Chestnut-backed Chickadees overlap with Mountain Chickadees, but are usually found in denser, wetter forest. They are much more common than Black-capped west of the Puget Trough. Like Black-capped, they are also at home among people, and the two species are seen together at bird feeders in Seattle and other westside cities . The common call is a *zitta-zitta-zee*; there is no whistled song.

Small and short-tailed. Dark brown cap and throat, rich chestnut back and sides. Dark sides a good mark when colors are not visible in poor light.

Boreal Chickadee

Poecile hudsonicus

L 5.5"   **WS** 8"

Look for this large, rather drab chickadee in Engelmann spruce
and lodgepole pine forests at high elevations in northern
Whatcom, Okanogan, Ferry and Pend Oreille Counties. Hart's
Pass, Chopaka Mountain, and Salmo Mountain are all good
places to look, although extensive forest fires have reduced
boreal habitat in some areas. Most foraging is high in lichen-
festooned trees. Call is a drawled *zhee zheee*, recognizably
chickadee-like.

Large and long-tailed.
Brown above, cinnamon
on sides. Brown cap,
restricted white cheek.

Bushtit

Psaltriparus minimus

L 4.5" | **WS** 6"

Bushtits might be too small to notice if they did not gather in winter flocks of up to 30 birds to roam through woodlands and suburbs. They move from shrub to shrub in a flowing line of tiny birds, and can cover a suet feeder with brown backs and tails. They also hang upside-down to search for insect eggs and larvae under leaves. Common residents in the western lowlands, they occur well up the river valleys into the foothills. They also extend up the Columbia River to Klickitat County, and are widespread along the upper and middle Yakima River. Birds in the isolated population at the Potholes Reservoir are entirely gray, typical of more southerly populations. Birds in flocks are in constant vocal contact with soft *ps ps ps* notes.

Very small, drab gray and brown songbird with tiny bill, long tail. Male has dark brown eyes. Female has pale yellow eyes.

Red-breasted Nuthatch

Sitta canadensis

L 4.5" | **WS** 8.5"

If you see a bird climbing head-down on a tree trunk, it's a nuthatch. Red-breasted is the most common and widespread Washington species, breeding in conifer and mixed woodlands throughout the state, even in isolated stands in farmland towns. They occur everywhere else during migration, including throughout the Columbia Basin, and are regulars at bird feeders. Adult and juvenile males have black caps, adult and juvenile females gray. Strident *ank ank ank* calls mark this bird's presence, often joining other small birds to harass a pygmy-owl or other predator.

Small; long-billed and short-tailed. Gray above and rusty below, with black cap and eye line and prominent white eyebrow. Female has gray cap. wing stripe.

White-breasted Nuthatch

Sitta carolinensis

L 6" | **WS** 11"

Fairly common and vividly conspicuous residents of dry
conifer forests on the east slope of the Cascades and eastward,
White-breasted Nuthatches inch their way up and down tree
trunks and branches, probing crevices with their long bills
and chipping away bark to get at their insect prey. They also
occur in oak woodland along the Lower Columbia River west
to Longview, where Ridgefield NWR is a good place to look.
As winter approaches, they forage with increasing intensity;
visiting feeders, they fly away with sunflower seeds to hoard
them in crevices. The quickly repeated calls are lower-pitched
and more musical than those of Red-breasted.

Larger than Red-breasted,
with longer bill. Gray above
and white below, with
narrow black cap and rusty
undertail. Females of all ages
have gray cap, males black.

Pygmy Nuthatch

Sitta pygmaea

L 4" | **WS** 8"

Pygmy Nuthatches are resident in ponderosa pine woodland on the lower east slopes of the Cascades and in the Northeastern Highlands and Blue Mountains. They move through the forest in flocks, in the nonbreeding season sometimes dozens of birds, and examine every cranny in the crowns of the pines. Unlike the White-breasted and Red-breasted Nuthatches, which forage on trunks and large limbs, Pygmy Nuthatches spend a great deal of time among smaller branches, twigs, needles, and cones. The Wenas Creek area has long been known for its Pygmy Nuthatches. The high-pitched chattering or peeping calls keep the flock together as it moves through the tree canopy.

Very small. Gray above and pale buff below, with brown cap and darker eye line.

Brown Creeper

Certhia americana

L 5" | **WS** 8"

Brown Creepers breed throughout the state's forests where there are mature trees, especially species with furrowed bark. In migration and winter, they are also found in wooded city parks and isolated groves in open country. This is the only bird likely to be mistaken for a falling leaf, as it drops from high in one tree to the base of the next; it slowly makes its way up the trunk and sometimes larger branches, only to flutter down and begin again. The sharp claws and pointed tail, much like those of woodpeckers, are for tree climbing. The call is a high-pitched double *seee-seee*, and the song is a complex series of similarly high notes.

Beautifully camouflaged; bark-colored above, snowy white below. Ascends trees with jerky motions. Bill slender, slightly curved.

Rock Wren
Salpinctes obsoletus

L 6" | **WS** 9"

This light-colored wren is a bird of rocky cliffs and talus slopes all over the eastside, even surprisingly small rock outcrops in the midst of other open habitats. A few breed in such habitats, even fairly high in the Cascades and Olympics, and a few are seen in migration and winter on jetties and other rocky substrates at the coast. Because insects are hard to find in the dry rocks during the winter, most are present only mid-April to October. The striking song is a long series of trilled and slurred segments, each different from the one before it. The high-pitched calls are also trilled. Listen for Rock Wrens at the Ginkgo Petrified Forest Interpretive Center.

Sandy brown, finely patterned wren, paler below and with rich buff belly. Long bill; short tail not cocked.

Canyon Wren

Catherpes mexicanus

L 6" | **WS** 7.5"

Canyon Wrens occur east of the Cascades and are usually found along rocky cliffs, in contrast with Rock Wrens that are talus dwellers. But they favor moister settings with more vegetation, usually in canyons near streams or lakes. They forage in fits and starts over the rocks like a chestnut nuthatch, their snow-white breast startling insects into giving away their presence. Because their habitat is more productive, Canyon Wrens can find enough food to spend the winter and are thus resident. The song is a beautiful series of descending slurred notes, louder and lower-pitched at each step. Call is a sharp *dzheet*, audible even near a waterfall and reminiscent of an American Dipper.

Strikingly colored, mostly chestnut wren with brown cap, snow-white throat and upper breast. Bright rusty, black-banded tail not cocked. Very long bill.

House Wren

Troglodytes aedon

L 5" | **WS** 6"

If you want to see a House Wren, put up a bird house; they
love them, especially when there are no woodpecker holes or
other natural cavities available. House Wrens are widespread
residents from late April to September in low-elevation dry
forest and riparian woodland with good shrub cover in the
interior and, locally, in the Puget Trough; they are uncommon
in and around Seattle. They occur much more sparingly west of
the Puget Trough, mostly as migrants. House Wrens forage low
among the shrubbery and along logs and branches. Males take a
higher perch to sing their rapid series of bubbling notes. Call is
a harsh, continuous chatter.

Plain brown wren, lighter below.
Faint pale eyebrow. Wings and
tail finely and heavily barred.
Tail often cocked.

Pacific Wren

Troglodytes pacificus

L 4" | **WS** 5.5"

Resident in dense, wet conifer and mixed forests throughout the state, these dark brown mites are almost mouselike in their foraging methods, creeping over the ground and fearlessly hopping into dark crevices among roots and in fallen hollow logs. They ascend only to sing. Each male may have up to 100 different song phrases, which he combines and recombines into an ever-changing six-second song; as the notes tumble out, the singer cocks his tail over his back and sways his head from side to side. Calls are kissing notes, usually doubled, often the best way to find these little wrens. Migrants from the north may turn up anywhere, even in the Columbia Basin.

Very small, dark wren. Faint pale eyebrow. Heavily barred wings, tail, and underparts. Quite short tail usually cocked. Often bobs up and down.

Marsh Wren

Cistothorus palustris

L 5" | **WS** 6"

Marsh Wrens are found throughout the year in cattail and bulrush marshes across the state. They skulk in the dense vegetation, but males ascend cattail stems to sing in full sight. The male builds several conspicuous globular nests to attract females; sometimes more than one nests in his territory. Occasional migrants are seen away from marshes. The male's long, complex song comprises different combinations of dozens of song phrases. Calls are repeated *chit chit chit*.

Rusty and buffy wren with brown cap and prominent white eyebrow. Distinctive black-and-white streaked back. Wings and tail barred, sides plain. Tail usually cocked.

Bewick's Wren

Thryomanes bewickii

L 5" | **WS** 7"

Formerly restricted to western Washington, with small populations along the Yakima River and its tributaries, in recent years this non-migratory species has colonized the eastside, mostly by traveling up river valleys. This is another species that prospers around humans, nesting in any sort of crevice it can find, even mailboxes, and visiting suet feeders. Like most wrens, and some sparrows and other birds of the underbrush, it cocks its tail as it forages in the shrubbery. The song is variable, often trilled, sometimes sounding rather like a Song Sparrow. Call is a soft series of *tik* notes.

Brown above and white below, with prominent white eyebrow. Long, heavily barred tail with much white along edges.

American Dipper

Cinclus mexicanus

L 7.5" | **WS** 11"

Dippers occur throughout Washington on the shores of swift streams and rivers in wooded country; some move to lake shores in winter. These uniquely aquatic songbirds forage for insects and small fish underwater. They float like a duck with their dense, waterproof plumage, then pop below the surface and swim with their wings. Their sharp claws let them walk on the bottom as well. Watch for the flash of the white lower eyelid, and look for their beautiful moss nests on boulders and under bridges. Nesting is early in spring. The musical song is loud enough to be heard over waterfowls and torrents, and the calls are equally loud, a series of *zheet* notes.

Compact dark gray bird, with short tail sometimes cocked. Constantly bobs up and down.

Golden-crowned Kinglet

Regulus satrapa

L 4" | **WS** 7"

Found throughout the state, Golden-crowned Kinglets are birds of wet conifer forests at all elevations. Some move into other habitats during migration and winter; it can be a shock to see a migrant foraging at eye level in sagebrush. Mostly in the canopy, they sometimes feed on the ground when temperatures are freezing and treetops are tossing in the wind. They move rapidly through the branches, and spend much time hovering to glean insect larvae and eggs from the undersides of needles and branches. The calls are a series of very high-pitched *see see see* notes, the song a more complex sequence at the same pitch.

Tiny, active bird with thin, short bill and striped head. Olive above, gray below, with colorful crown outlined in black. Whitish eyebrow and dusky eye stripe. Greenish-edged wing with one white bar bordered black behind. Thin dark legs with yellow toes. Male's crown yellow and orange, female's yellow.

Ruby-crowned Kinglet

Regulus calendula

L 4" | **WS** 7.5"

Ruby-crowned Kinglets forage frenetically with flicking wings, gleaning small insects from leaves and branches. They also visit sapsucker holes at any time of year. They breed in conifer forests from the Cascade crest east through the Northeastern Highlands and in the Blue Mountains. Unlike Golden-crowns, they desert their breeding habitat to winter in mixed woodland and lowland brush throughout much of the state; at that time they may be in mixed flocks with very similar Hutton's Vireos. They are also common migrants everywhere. The song starts high, like a Golden-crown's, then descends into a surprisingly loud series of low-pitched warbled notes. Watch a singing male to see the hidden crown patch suddenly burst into flaming view. Call is a double *di-dit*.

Tiny, active bird with thin, short bill and rather plain head. Olive above and gray below, with white eye ring. Greenish-edged tail and wing; rear wing bar bordered black behind. Thin, dark legs with yellow toes. Male with hidden bright red crown patch.

Townsend's Solitaire

Myadestes townsendi

L 8.5" | **WS** 14.5"

Townsend's Solitaires are birds of open forest throughout Washington's mountains, including the Olympics, from mid-April to mid-September. They are seen widely in migration all over the state March–April and September–October, and a few birds winter, usually in native or introduced junipers. Insect-eaters during the breeding season, solitaires turn to fruit in winter, and juniper berries are a significant winter food. They often nest in a hollow in a cut bank over a road or trail. The song is a long, emphatic series of finch-like warbled notes, sometimes given in flight. The call is a single bell-like note, somewhat like the toot of a Northern Pygmy-Owl.

Slender gray thrush with prominent white eye ring. Buffy wing patches not always visible, but conspicuous in flight, as are white edges to long tail.

Western Bluebird

Sialia mexicana

L 7" | **WS** 13.5"

Western Bluebirds are locally common summer visitors
March–August east of the Cascades, primarily in openings
in the ponderosa pine zone. They also occur westside in open
woodland and forest edge. Their numbers are limited by the
availability of nest cavities, and they declined greatly in the
twentieth century, but nest box programs, such as those at
Joint Base Lewis McChord and on San Juan Island, have
helped re-establish the species in many places. They can be
seen almost anywhere in migration, and have wintered locally
in the western lowlands. More elaborate versions of the musical
chew and *chirew* calls serve as the male's spring song.

Short-tailed, with upright
posture. Male bright blue
above, with rusty breast and
sides. Female (below) with blue
primarily on wings, rump, and
tail, some on head and
upperparts. Much rusty color
on breast and sides.

Mountain Bluebird

Sialia currucoides

L 7" | **WS** 14"

This is the bluebird of open areas east, from alpine meadows in all mountain ranges to grasslands around the Columbia Basin, wherever there are old woodpecker holes, cliff crevices, or other nest cavities. Mountain Bluebirds are uncommon spring migrants and winter visitors west. They arrive in March and move up into the mountains later, then depart by the end of October. They profit greatly from nest boxes erected along "bluebird trails," such as the one along Umptanum Road southwest of Ellensburg. Like Western Bluebirds, Mountain Bluebirds forage for insects in low vegetation and on the ground, even hovering like tiny kestrels. They also eat berries when they are in season. Mellow musical phrases such as *chup*, *cheep*, and *chuwerr* are given as calls and interspersed in song.

Male bright blue all over, paler on belly. Blue paler than in male Western. Female (below) brown with blue wings and tail, only faint hint of rusty below.

Veery
Catharus fuscescens

L 7" | **WS** 12"

Veeries are common breeders, mid-May through August, in riparian woodland and broadleaf forest at lower elevations in the ponderosa pine zone on the east side of the Cascades and in the foothills of the Northeast Highlands and Blue Mountains. They feed like other thrushes on insects and fruits. These reddish, rather plain-looking thrushes are not easy to see in dense vegetation, but follow your ears. The song is a beautiful series of descending fluty notes, *veeur veeur veeur veeur,* and the call is a short version of one of those notes.

Reddish-brown upperparts and white to gray underparts. Lightly marked breast and gray sides distinctive.

Swainson's Thrush

Catharus ustulatus

L 7" | **WS** 12"

Swainson's is the most common of the three spotted thrushes
in Washington, generally breeding at higher elevations than
Veeries and lower than Hermits, but overlapping with both.
Swainson's Thrushes breed throughout the state's wetter forests
May–September, and are common migrants everywhere west;
they are only rarely seen in the Columbia Basin. They forage
for insects in shrubs and on the ground, but take more fruit
when berries appear in summer. Birds east of the Cascades are
distinctly less rusty above than those west of the Cascades. The
song consists of an ascending series of fluty, almost ethereal
notes. Calls are a soft *whit* and an odd, electronic *rhee*.

Olive-brown to reddish-brown
upperparts, moderately heavily
spotted breast. Buffy eye ring
and brown sides characteristic.

Hermit Thrush

Catharus guttatus

L 7" | **WS** 11.5"

Hermit Thrushes are the most likely of the three spotted thrushes to be seen in migration anywhere in the state April–May and September–November. They also winter in small numbers throughout the western lowlands, especially near the coast, where they feed on wax myrtle berries. A few winter in the interior where fruits are available. They breed in higher-elevation conifer forests in all of the mountain ranges from late May through August. The Hermit's beautiful song begins with a pure note, followed by a series of fluty notes on one pitch. Subsequent songs alter the pitch of the introductory note. The calls are a soft *tchup* and an upslurred nasal *vreeeh*.

Brown back, with rusty wings and especially tail. Heavily spotted breast and gray sides. Lacks prominent eye ring. Often droops wings and cocks tail.

American Robin

Turdus migratorius

L 10" | **WS** 17"

Robins are ubiquitous residents, breeding in cities and towns, even in the driest and most open parts of the state. They occur in all wooded habitats with openings, from the coast up to treeline. They have even nested in open sagebrush. The earth-worm-eating birds of your yard disappear in fall to join small flocks that roam the countryside through the winter looking for fruiting trees such as hawthorn, mountain ash, and holly. On the eastside, thousands winter in apple orchards with unpicked fruit, roosting in dense conifers. The song is a rollicking series of sprightly whistles with a back-and-forth cadence. Calls are a sharp *pip pip* and, perhaps as a flight contact call, a sibilant *sweeweep*.

Familiar large, red-breasted thrush with yellow bill. Broken white eye ring, white throat with dark streaks, white undertail coverts, white tail corners. Male darker overall than female, with black head. Female paler overall than male, with brown head.

Varied Thrush

Ixoreus naevius

L 9.5" | **WS** 16"

Varied Thrushes breed throughout the mountains of the state in wet conifer forests, locally down to sea level on the west-side. Fall finds them migrating downslope to winter widely in wooded parts of the state. Their primary foraging method is to flip over leaves and twigs with their bill and capture whatever invertebrates they find. They also pick up seeds and suet that drop from bird feeders visited by other species. Like American Robins, they also come to fruiting trees in fall and winter. The song is a haunting series of long, level, almost electronic notes, each on a different pitch. The call is a soft *tchup*.

Vivid buffy wing markings unlike plain wings of slightly larger American Robin. Male strikingly marked blue-gray and rusty orange. Bright eyebrow, black breast band. Female patterned like male but less colorful, with gray on head and breast band.

Gray Catbird
Dumetella carolinensis

L 8.5" | **WS** 11"

Catbirds migrate from lower latitudes to breed in Washington mid-May to September. They are found in dense riparian and deciduous growth at lower elevations on the east slope of the Cascades and in the Northeastern Highlands and Blue Mountains. A few have bred in the western lowlands. They spend much of their time low in shrubs or on the ground, feeding on insects and fruits, and are often detected by their nasal, catlike calls. The song is a series of simple phrases, from musical to harsh, given continuously over long periods. A good look at a catbird includes a view of the chestnut patch under the tail.

Dark gray with black cap, long tail. Tail often cocked.

Sage Thrasher

Oreoscoptes montanus

L 8.5" | **WS** 12"

The well-named Sage Thrasher breeds in sagebrush/bunchgrass habitats throughout the Columbia Basin, where it is present from late March to mid-September. Those habitats and the birds in them have been much reduced by the spread of agriculture, but thrashers are still locally common. They forage mostly on the ground, and are often seen running between shrubs. When singing their varied warbled song, which may continue for up to several minutes, they usually perch conspicuously on a sagebrush. The display is a wild, careening flight, up and down and around and around, then back onto another sagebrush with wings up. Alarm call is a short *chuk*.

Sandy brown above, heavily streaked below. Bright yellow-orange eyes.

European Starling

Sturnus vulgaris

L 8.5" | **WS** 16"

Non-native starlings became established in Washington in the 1950s, and are now residents throughout the state everywhere but in dense forests. After breeding, they feed in large flocks in open country, moving through a field with birds in the back flying to the front in constant rollover. They roost in trees and under bridges by the thousands, and amaze onlookers with the fluid murmurations of their flocks as they come to roost. Spring birds are beautifully iridescent. City starlings nest in streetlights and other crevices, and take over woodpecker holes by sheer persistence. Their amazing songs are full of chuckles, rattles, and tweets, and include mimicry of of a surprising variety of sounds, from bird songs to mechanical noise. The harsh calls of juveniles insisting to be fed are a sign of summer.

Long, pointed bill and short tail. Pointed wings. Iridescent green and purple. Fresh plumage (above left) in fall and winter heavily spangled with pale chevrons, looking spotted at a distance; bill dark. Pale feather tips and edges wear off over the winter, revealing the stunning colors of spring birds (above right). Juvenile (below left) plain brown all over. Molt into adult plumage begins quickly and produces more and more white spangles as summer goes on..

Bohemian Waxwing

Bombycilla garrulus

L 8" | **WS** 14.5"

Waxwings seem to be the smoothest of birds, with perfectly fitting feathers. The expanded tips of some secondaries look like red wax, and are important in indicating age and status to other flock members. Bohemian Waxwings have bred a few times in the North Cascades, but are mostly visitors from the boreal forest November–February. Most appear in eastern Washington, where fruiting trees in towns and cities and unpicked fruit in orchards feed them well. Every few years small numbers invade the westside, to the excitement of birders there. They are best found by looking for trees still holding fruit during the winter, including hawthorns, crabapples, and introduced mountain ash. The calls are lower-pitched versions of the high *seeeee* calls of Cedar Waxwings, with a distinct trilling quality.

Gray-brown, with prominent crest and yellow-tipped tail. Red "wax" droplets at ends of secondaries. White and yellow in wings and chestnut undertail coverts are characteristic. In flight, the size and shape of European Starling.

Cedar Waxwing

Bombycilla cedrorum

L 7" | **WS** 12"

Cedar Waxwings are consummate fruit-eaters. They flock to fruiting trees over much of the year, leaving the flocks only to raise a family. They prefer open woodlands of any type, especially those with a good supply of berries in fall and winter. They are distinctly more common from mid-May to mid-October on the westside, with larger numbers wintering east, where they often feed on unpicked grapes and apples in the same trees as Bohemians. They have no song, but give very frequent high-pitched *seeeee* calls, perhaps a way to keep flocks together.

Yellowish belly and lack of white and yellow in wings distinguish this species from Bohemian. Immatures of both species lack "wax" on the secondaries; juveniles of both have streaked underparts.

House Sparrow

Passer domesticus

L 6" | **WS** 9.5"

House Sparrows, representatives of an Old World family not closely related to our native sparrows, were introduced into North America from Europe in the 1850s and spread across the continent to reach Washington in 1895. They thrive in urban and agricultural areas, habitats that are expanding, but House Sparrow populations are decreasing in many parts of their American range. They usually nest in crevices, but small colonies may also build untidy spherical nests in trees. The song is a series of loud notes best described as *chirp*, probably the origin of that word. Males in spring accompany their chirping with a vigorous dancing display.

Male's bill black, head multicolored with strong black throat and upper breast. Upperparts rich chestnut, with black streaks and single strong white wingbar. In nonbreeding season, bill brown and yellow.

Female differs from native sparrows by shorter tail, buffy eyebrow, and pair of broad buffy stripes down back. Plain underparts.

American Pipit

Anthus rubescens

L 6.5" | **WS** 10.5"

Pipits are open-country birds, with long hind claws and the habit of walking rather than hopping. They lack the intricate face pattern and largely black tail of Horned Larks, with which they may associate. American Pipits migrate throughout the state, and winter locally west in places such as the Samish and Skagit Flats. They also breed in small numbers in the alpine and subalpine zone of the Olympics and Cascades, usually near water. The song is a long series of sweet *tsip* notes given by males in flight over their territory, accelerating during the jerky, stairstep descent. Birds in flight, often in flocks, call see-*SEEP*, sounding something like "pipit."

Nonbreeding and immature birds sparrowlike, but with thin bill, walking gait, and wagging tail. Muted brown above, buffier below with fine streaks. Breeding adult richer buff below, with fewer streaks.

Evening Grosbeak

Coccothraustes vespertinus

L 8" | **WS** 14"

Evening Grosbeaks occur statewide in both broadleaf and conifer forests, but their appearances are difficult to predict. They are irruptive, appearing in numbers for a while and then disappearing. They breed, migrate, and winter widely, but their presence at any place and time is not guaranteed. They breed most abundantly where there are spruce budworm outbreaks in mountain conifer forests. They also visit cities and towns, especially in spring, to feed on tree buds and sunflower seeds at feeders. Evening Grosbeaks are noisy, especially in flocks, with a series of *cheeep* calls, some of them pure whistles, others burry.

Finch with huge pale bill, short tail. Male brown and golden all over, with yellow eyebrows, black wings and tail, and much white on inner wing. First-year birds have much brown overlaying that white. Female (right) mostly sandy brown, with little yellow. Black wings and tail with white patches.

Pine Grosbeak

Pinicola enucleator

L 9" | **WS** 14.5"

Pine Grosbeaks are widely distributed but uncommon residents of high-elevation conifer forests in the Olympics, Cascades, Northeastern Highlands, and Blue Mountains. Small numbers wander to the adjacent lowlands in winter, more regularly in eastern than in western Washington. They are rarely seen in the lower parts of the Columbia Basin, and are absent from the southwestern counties west of the Cascades. The best way to find them in winter in the lowlands is to search fruiting trees where there are robins and waxwings. The rich, warbled song may include mimicry of other species and two-noted *chee-vlee* flight calls.

Large finch with arched bill. Strong white wingbars. Body size of Evening Grosbeak, but long tail makes the entire bird almost as long as a robin. Male gray with variable amounts of reddish pink.

Female gray, with saffron on head, rump, and sometimes breast.

Gray-crowned Rosy-Finch

Leucosticte tephrocotis

L 6" | **WS** 13"

Rosy-finches are birds of extremes, breeding in harsh arctic and alpine environments inhabited by few other birds. This species nests in rock crevices in alpine areas of the Cascades and Olympics. Flocks drop down October–November to winter at lower elevations in and around the Columbia Basin, primarily where there are cliffs. In Grand, Moses, and Frenchman Coulees, they roost in rock crevices and Cliff Swallow nests, foraging on nearby prairies for grass and forb seeds. Birds from farther north are easily distinguished in these flocks, as they are gray only above the eyes. The call is a buzzy *chew*, somewhat like a House Sparrow. The song strings together similar notes into a longer series.

Rich brown with overtones of rosy or pink, especially on underparts and wings. Head of Washington's breeding adults largely gray, with black crown and throat. Immature like adult but with darker head. Juvenile brown all over, with salmon patches in wings.

House Finch
Haemorhous mexicanus

L 6" | **WS** 9.5"

House Finches thrive in hot, dry climates. A century ago they were limited to south-central Washington, but with forest clearing, agriculture, and urbanization, they now occupy the entire lowlands of the state. They thrive around humans, nesting in hanging plants and bringing their young to bird feeders as soon as they fledge. A small number of males are yellow rather than red; those birds' food has not supplied sufficient carotenoids, the pigments that produce red in feathers. The song is a sprightly warble, usually ending in a buzz, and the call is a musical ascending *sweet*.

Sparrow-sized finch with fairly long tail, arched bill. Male brown with red or pinkish markings on head, breast, and rump. Heavily streaked belly.

Female brown with brown-streaked underparts. Arched bill and long tail help distinguish House Finch from other red finches.

Purple Finch
Haemorhous purpureus

L 6" | **WS** 10"

Adult male Purple Finches are red, not purple. This species is a bird of the forests of western Washington and the lower east side of the Cascades, typical of deciduous and riparian woodland rather than urban or suburban areas. If you live in the woods, expect Purple, not House Finches, at your feeders. They favor fruiting trees of all sorts in fall. Males in their first year are brown like females, but commonly sing. The song is a rich and pretty warble, the calls a sharp *tip* and a whistled *chew-lee*.

Large bill, somewhat arched. Tail prominently notched. Male largely red, much paler on belly.

Head seems large compared with House Finch's. Female and first-year male brown above; heavily streaked below, with unstreaked undertail coverts. Pale supercilium and malar stripe.

Cassin's Finch

Haemorhous cassinii

L 6" | **WS** 11.5"

Cassin's Finches breed in dry mountain forests from the
Cascades crest east. They abound in ponderosa pine and
Douglas-fir forests, but also occur up to treeline in more open
spruce/fir stands. They overlap with Purple Finches where
conifer stands border riparian strips, and sometimes feed
with them, for example in Manastash Canyon. Except in years
with bountiful conifer seed crops, most depart in winter. As in
Purple Finches, first-year males look like females but also sing.
The loud, warbled song has much variation, including mimicry
of other species. Calls are a slurred, whistled *wheeyou* and a
dry *tidilip*.

Bill a bit more sharply pointed than in
similar Purple Finch. Male has bright red,
unmarked crown. Belly mostly white,
unmarked.

Female like Purple Finch but streaks darker,
finer, more sharply defined. Undertail
coverts streaked.

Common Redpoll

Acanthis flammea

L 5" | **WS** 9"

They do not visit Washington every winter, but in years when seed crops are insufficient on their arctic and subarctic breeding grounds, Common Redpolls come south in numbers. They are sometimes locally common November–February from the Cascades east, mostly at lower elevations. They invade the westside even less frequently, keeping to the northern counties. They feed on the seeds of birches and alders, often with gold-finches and siskins and hanging upside down like other small finches. They also feed on weed seeds in open fields. They have chattering calls and drawn-out nasal whistles rising in pitch.

Very small finch with tiny yellow bill. Male with red crown, red wash on breast, coarse streaks on sides. Female darker and more heavily streaked, lacks red on breast.

Red Crossbill

Loxia curvirostra

L 6" | **WS** 11"

A feeding crossbill perches on a conifer cone, opens each scale with its crossed mandibles, and plucks the seed out with its tongue. Various populations of Red Crossbill differ in size, bill size, and calls, that variation correlated with which conifer species they specialize in, whether pines, spruces, hemlocks, or Douglas-firs. Crossbills are very irregular in occurrence, common at times and then disappearing as cone crops wax and wane. The calls, often given in flight, are loud single or double chips, which differ between populations. Songs are complex and variable combinations of whistles and trills, often incorporating flight calls.

Prominently crossed bill varies greatly in size in different populations. Long, pointed wings and short, notched tail. Adult male's brick-red plumage is often mixed with yellowish; some tend to orange. Brightest on head, underparts, and rump.

Female brown, variably washed greenish to yellow. Juvenile of both sexes streaked.

White-winged Crossbill

Loxia leucoptera

L 6.5" | **WS** 10.5"

White-winged Crossbills do not winter in Washington every year, but large numbers occasionally invade from the north to roam the conifer forests of the northern mountains; they are much more rarely seen in the lowlands both west and east. Birds have at times lingered through the summer, but there are no definite breeding records for the state. They feed primarily on spruce seeds, but can also be seen at larch, hemlock, and Douglas-fir cones. The song is a series of harsh trills and chipping notes. The *chiff chiff* calls are similar to those of redpolls.

Crossed mandibles evident except in young juveniles. Black wings with broad white wingbars, black tail. Male (aobve) bright pinkish-red, colors purer than in Red Crossbill. Female (right) greenish, with wings and tail like male's. Faint streaks on underparts.

Pine Siskin

Spinus pinus

L 5" | **WS** 9"

Pine Siskins are common and widespread in some years and scarce to absent from many areas in others. They inhabit conifer and mixed forests from sea level to high in the mountains. On the westside in winter, flocks move through the forest searching for red alder cones, spending hours extracting the seeds. They also take seeds from conifer cones and herbaceous plants, even out in the open. They readily come to feeders, especially those offering thistle seed. They communicate with a high-pitched rising *zeeeeeeee* and chattering notes. The song is a complex mixture of chirps, warbles, and squeaks.

Small, heavily streaked finch with slender bill. Variable amount of yellow in wings and tail, independent of sex and age.

Lesser Goldfinch

Spinus psaltria

L 4.5" | **WS** 8"

Limited just a few decades ago to oak woodlands in southern Klickitat County, Lesser Goldfinches have steadily spread north, and are now resident wherever there are trees from the Vancouver area across the southern edge of the Columbia Basin to Walla Walla and beyond, and north in the Puget Trough to Tacoma. The Lyle area and Lyons Ferry Park are good locations. They are a straggler to the rest of the state, where they are often seen at thistle feeders with American Goldfinches and siskins. Calls include a short chatter and musical *tink-oo*, often given in flight; the song is a drawn-out series of varied phrases, some musical and some not.

Very small finch with white patch at base of primaries. Male has black cap, greenish back, and yellow underparts.

Female entirely greenish, paler below. Primary patch reduced but usually visible. White wing bars and edgings not as conspicuous as in American. Bill dark above, pale below.

American Goldfinch

Spinus tristis

L 5" | **WS** 9"

The state bird of Washington, the American Goldfinch is a common breeder throughout the lowlands, nesting late in spring when there are abundant thistle seeds to feed their nestlings. They nest in trees and feed in open areas, a combination they find at forest edges. Winter flocks of birds in dull, nonbreeding plumage travel widely across open country; they are more common at this season in eastern than western Washington. The song is a complex warble of musical notes. The call, given most frequently in flight, is a musical *per-chic-o-ree* or *potato-chip*.

Small finch. Black wings with white wingbars and white-edged secondaries; black tail with white spots. Male in breeding plumage (above) bright yellow with black crown, yellow-orange bill. Breeding female (not shown) dull yellow all over, whiter on lower belly Nonbreeding adult (right) pale sandy with yellowish head; male with more brightly patterned wings than female.

Lapland Longspur

Calcarius lapponicus

L 6" | **WS** 11.5"

Lapland Longspurs appear on the outer coast in migration, with more found September–October than in May. They are more widespread as migrants in the open country of the Columbia Basin, where a few stay through the winter, often flocking with Horned Larks or Snow Buntings. The Waterville Plateau is a good site. These are birds of open spaces, feeding in small flocks on interior prairies, coastal sand dunes, and salt marshes. When flushed, they fly high, and often disappear into the distance, a behavior that distinguishes them from sparrows, most of which fly up and land nearby. Birds in flight give a rattling call interspersed with *tew* notes.

Breeding-plumaged male streaked above, with vivid black head markings and rusty hindneck. White below, with black-streaked sides. Female with dark-outlined brown cheek patches and hint of rusty on hindneck.

Nonbreeding birds sparrowlike, but with longer wings with rusty-edged secondaries and coverts. Buffy underparts with streaked sides. Cheek patch with dark outline distinctive.

Snow Bunting

Plectrophenax nivalis

L 7" | **WS** 14"

Snow Buntings come from the Arctic to visit our prairies and beaches from November to April, often in small flocks. They are more common on the eastside, especially in the northern parts of the Columbia Basin, where hundreds sometimes gather on the Waterville and Timentwa Plateaus and in the Okanogan Highlands. On the westside, they usually appear on the outer coast or in the northern Puget Trough. In the interior, they often associate with Horned Larks and longspurs, but are easily distinguished by their big white wing patches. Flight calls are mostly sweet whistles.

Nonbreeding plumage sparrowlike, with much white on head. Light to medium-brown above with streaked back; white below with rusty-brown breast crescent. Wings heavily marked but with large white patches visible in flight; wing patches larger in male. Short bill yellow in winter.

Green-tailed Towhee

Pipilo chlorurus

L 7"   **WS** 10"

Green-tailed Towhees breed in small numbers on the western side of the Blue Mountains. Biscuit Ridge Road is an excellent area to search for them May–August, and a few have been seen at the Wenatchee Guard Station. They are usually on dry, shrubby hillsides, and are associated with mountain mahogany in many parts of their range. The birds are shy, but listen for their varied warbled song, much like that of a Fox Sparrow but with more trills. The call is a nasal *myaaah*, rather similar to that of the Spotted Towhee but slightly ascending, less harsh, and even more catlike.

Long-tailed sparrow with gray body, greenish wings and tail. Bright chestnut crown and distinct white throat.

Spotted Towhee

Pipilo maculatus

L 8.5" | **WS** 10.5"

Spotted Towhees are common lowland residents of dense shrub habitats throughout the state, from forest edge in the west to open hillsides in the east. Eastside birds are much more heavily spotted with white above, and females are paler; they are also more likely to migrate, with wintering birds primarily in the southern Columbia Basin and Columbia River Gorge. Towhees unearth seeds and insects by jumping into the air and scratching the ground with both feet simultaneously; this "double scratch" is easy to see when they are feeding nearby. The song is a harsh trill, fast enough to be called a buzz. The call is a descending whine, vaguely catlike.

Large, vividly marked sparrow with bright red eyes. Head and upperparts black. Scapulars and wings spotted white; tail with white tips and edges. More white on interior birds, less on coastal birds like this one. Sides extensively rusty, middle of underparts white. Female dark brown rather than black.

American Tree Sparrow

Spizelloides arborea

L 6" | **WS** 9.5"

These sturdy sparrows, visitors from subarctic breeding grounds, are present at shrubby forest edges in Washington from mid-October through March, when they occur throughout the open country east of the Cascades, often in small flocks. Common west, they are usually spotted somewhere in the Puget Trough. They feed in the open on seeds of forbs and grasses, but retire to dense thickets when disturbed. Russian olive is a favorite tree. Birds in flocks give a variety of *tseet* and *tew* calls.

Long-tailed sparrow marked with rich light brown and chestnut; narrow reddish head stripes. Dark spot on plain breast. Conspicuous white wingbars.

Chipping Sparrow
Spizella passerina

L 5.5" | **WS** 8.5"

Chipping Sparrows breed widely in forests, except the wettest ones, at all elevations on the eastside. They also occur locally on the westside in drier habitats such as oak woodlands on the San Juan Islands, the northeast edge of the Olympic Peninsula, and the Tacoma Prairies. Present April–September, they head to the southwestern US and northwestern Mexico for the winter. The streaked juvenile plumage is retained through the first fall migration, when they can be common in open subalpine habitats. The song is a long, dry trill, the calls *tsit* or *tseet*.

Small, long-tailed sparrow with heavily patterned sandy brown back; two inconspicuous white wing bars. Adult in breeding plumage with bright rusty cap, white eyebrow, black eye line; underparts light gray, throat paler.

Juvenile has paler bill; head with brown streaks, heavily streaked underparts. Retains this plumage into fall.

Brewer's Sparrow

Spizella breweri

L 5.5" | **WS** 7.5"

This species is common wherever sagebrush with native bunchgrass persists in eastern Washington; it is now rare at lower elevations in much of the southern Columbia Basin. In June and July, when the streaked juveniles fledge, the birds may move into other, usually moister, open-country habitats, especially near springs. By the end of August, as the landscape gets drier and less productive, they are gone, some moving up to the subalpine to join flocks of migrating Chipping Sparrows. When flushed, they look small, pale, and long-tailed. The ear-pleasing long song of a Brewer's Sparrow is one of the characteristic sounds of the shrub steppe in April and May, an often lengthy series of trills at different speeds and on different pitches. The call is a weak chip note resembling that of a Chipping Sparrow.

Small, long-tailed, generally drab sparrow. Sandy brown upperparts heavily streaked with darker brown, including crown. Plain underparts.

Vesper Sparrow

Pooecetes gramineus

L 6" | **WS** 10"

The Vesper is a common and widespread sparrow of the shrub steppe and dry to moist grasslands of the interior April–September. Small and declining populations nest at remnant prairies and small airports in the Puget Trough. More than twice the bulk of Brewer's and with a shorter tail, Vesper Sparrows show white outer tail feathers as they fly up from the roadside. The beautiful song is two or more musical *teeeur* notes followed by trilled segments. "Vesper" refers to evening, when they are said to sing especially sweetly. When singing in spring, males of both Brewer's and Vesper Sparrows perch on sagebrush or fence wires, much the easiest way to see them. Call is a sharp chirp.

Heavily streaked above, lightly streaked below. Head rather plain, showing conspicuous white eye ring. Rusty lesser coverts may be visible. Only heavily streaked sparrow with white outer tail feathers, obvious in flight.

Lark Sparrow

Chondestes grammacus

L 6.5" | **WS** 11"

These strikingly marked sparrows are characteristic of drier sagebrush habitats, where they are present mid-April through September, though less common than Brewer's and Vesper. They also occur in agricultural areas with scattered trees, into which they may fly when disturbed, unlike other open-country sparrows. They also fly farther than other sparrows at such times, in long undulating sweeps with the white border of the tail very conspicuous. In courtship displays, the male struts around like a little turkey with wings drooped and tail raised. The song is a series of trills and harsh *churr* phrases. Call is a sharp metallic *tink*.

Vivid head pattern of black, white, and chestnut distinctive. Plain-breasted, with dark spot in middle; similar spot only in very different American Tree and Sagebrush Sparrows. Only brown sparrow with so much white on tail.

Sagebrush Sparrow

Artemisiospiza nevadensis

L 6" | **WS** 8"

Sagebrush Sparrows are the most uncommon and local of the sparrows breeding in the shrub steppe; in many areas, invasive cheat grass now covers the open ground they require. The Quilomene WA and Moses Coulee are still dependable places to find them. They run like little roadrunners across expanses of bare ground, with the black underside of the tail conspicuous. They are early breeders, present from March through early August, when their habitat produces the most insects to feed the young. The song is brief, tinkling, and somewhat burry. Call is a short, junco-like *tsip*.

Plain gray head with white stripes contrasts with sandy-brown, finely streaked back. Underparts mostly unmarked except for prominent black breast spot. Slender tail mostly dark, with narrow white edges.

Savannah Sparrow

Passerculus sandwichensis

L 5.5" | **WS** 7"

This is the common sparrow of moist grasslands all over Washington, ascending even into high mountain meadows. It is very widespread east, and absent only from large areas of mostly forested lands west. Savannah Sparrows are one of the most common migrants in the state, found anywhere in open country; they winter locally in small numbers west, with even fewer wintering east. Size is variable, with larger birds coming down in winter from the Aleutian Islands. The song consists of a few introductory notes followed by a long, high-pitched musical buzz. Calls are single high-pitched *tsip* notes.

Heavily streaked sparrow with relatively short, notched tail. Much yellow on face characteristic. Streaks vary from black to medium brown. Streaks often form central breast spot.

Grasshopper Sparrow

Ammodramus savannarum

L 5" | **WS** 8"

Present in the Columbia Basin from mid–April through mid–August, the Grasshopper Sparrow is most common in slightly moister tracts of grassland, from wide-open prairie to shrub steppe with open grassy areas. Males sing from elevated perches and are usually visible when singing; otherwise, this skulking ground feeder is not easy to see. The unmusical, grass-hopper-like buzzy song *tik-tik-zeeeee* is difficult to hear except at close range. A second song, this one also given in flight, is a long series of short buzzy notes that sounds more like a Savannah Sparrow's song. Calls are short, staccato double or triple notes, inaudible to many observers.

Large-billed, flat-headed, short-tailed sparrow. Back beautifully patterned in reddish and brown, with fine pale streaks. Black-spotted wing coverts distinctive. Underparts buff, lores yellow. Legs seem long because of short tail.

Fox Sparrow

Passerella iliaca

L 7" | **WS** 10.5"

Washington has two different-looking populations of breeding Fox Sparrows. Dark brown, heavily marked birds, known as Sooty Fox Sparrows, breed in shrubby patches from Tatoosh Island south to Point Grenville on the outer coast and locally in the San Juan Islands. Migrant Sooties from the north winter in thickets over most of the state September–April. Gray-headed birds, known as Slate-colored Fox Sparrows, breed in shrubby openings in mountain conifer forests from the east slope of the Cascades east; most leave the state after September. Like towhees, Fox Sparrows forage on the ground with double-scratches. The rich song combines sweet whistles and buzzy trills. Call is a sharp *chip*.

Large sparrow, with reddish wings and tail, yellow lower mandible; underparts marked with chevrons rather than streaks, sometimes clustering into a central spot. Sooty Fox Sparrow medium to dark brown; plain-backed and plain-headed.

Slate-colored Fox Sparrow with gray head and back; markings on underparts usually darker and narrower than in Sooty, and lower mandible not as bright.

Song Sparrow

Melospiza melodia

L 6" | **WS** 8"

Song Sparrows are one of the most common resident birds in western Washington, from forest edges to suburbs. There is scarcely a bird feeder without them, as long as there are patches of shrubbery for nesting and no outdoor cats in the vicinity. On the eastside, they are more confined to riparian and wetland habitats as breeding birds, but occur more widely in moister terrestrial habitats in winter. More westerly breeding birds are darker and redder than those in the Columbia Basin and east. The song is a series of sprightly phrases, usually including a distinctive *tsink tsink tsee*. Call a low *chunk*, very different from the notes of other sparrows.

Long tail often cocked. Streaks on breast usually coalesce into a prominent central spot. From east side of Cascades west, quite reddish, with blurry streaks on sides. Interior birds (not shown) are slightly smaller and more brightly marked, with finer, more contrasting markings.

Lincoln's Sparrow
Melospiza lincolnii

L 6" | **WS** 7.5"

A bubbly, House Wren-like song coming from a mountain marsh or bog from the Cascades east indicates the presence of a Lincoln's Sparrow. This species occurs statewide in migration in shrubby areas; it winters in small numbers throughout the westside, less commonly east. Smaller and paler than Song Sparrows, Lincoln's Sparrows are even more skulking, but can be observed with persistence. Call a low-pitched *chip* or *smack*.

Smaller and paler than rather similar Song Sparrow, with grayer head and distinct eye ring. Breast and sides with buffy wash. Streaks of underparts finer but, like Song, at times including a central spot.

Golden-crowned Sparrow
Zonotrichia atricapilla

L 7" | **WS** 9.5"

Golden-crowned Sparrows are common migrants throughout the state, east to the eastern base of the Cascades; they are less common farther east. They are also common mid–September to mid–May on the westside, and winter in small numbers on the eastside, especially in the Yakima area. Wintering Golden-crowneds often occur in mixed flocks with White-crowneds and other sparrows, feeding on seeds out in the open but disappearing into the shrubbery at any disturbance. Golden-crowneds sing before they migrate north to British Columbia and Alaska to breed, a long whistled note followed by series of shorter and lower-pitched ones, oh dear me. Common call is a flat *tchup*, quite different from the White-crowned's call.

Slightly larger and darker than White-crowned, with similar color and shape. Breeding-plumaged adult has yellow crown outlined with broad black stripes.

Immature brown with dark bill; finely streaked crown often shows some yellowish.

White-crowned Sparrow

Zonotrichia leucophrys

L 7" | **WS** 9"

Three populations of this species inhabit Washington. "Puget Sound" White-crowned breed throughout the western lowlands and up into the Cascades, even through the passes onto the east side. In a few of the mountain locations, they actually occur together with "Gambel's" White-crowned, boreal forest breeders that are abundant throughout the state in migration and locally common in winter. At higher elevations in the Northeastern Highlands and Blue Mountains, there are breeding populations of "Mountain" White-crowned. The song is a series of whistled notes, *see see pretty pretty meeee* in Puget Sound and more varied in Gambel's. Call a soft *tick*.

Adult. Black and white (or gray) head stripes and plain underparts distinctive. Puget Sound population browner, with back streaks dark brown on lighter brown. Bill yellowish, not bright.

Gambel's brighter and grayer, back streaks rufous on gray. Bill usually rather bright orange.

First year. Like adult but head stripes rufous and gray-brown.

Dark-eyed Junco

Junco hyemalis

L 6" | **WS** 9"

Dark-eyed Juncos are sparrows, as indicated by their streaked juveniles, that have become very social and evolved bold color patterns. These patterns are important when they display to one another in flocks, each of which has a well-established dominance hierarchy. Watch them at your feeder to see one chase after another, with white tail feathers flared. They breed in forested landscapes all over the state, spreading out in winter to more open habitats. They are becoming more common in the largest cities, breeding in forested parks and yards. Occasional birds of the northern Slate-colored population can be found in winter flocks. The song is a long trill, more musical than that of a Chipping Sparrow. Calls are sharp *tip* notes.

Bright pink bill, prominent white outer tail feathers. Adult male with black hood, rusty back, pinkish sides. Winterers from more northerly populations with uniformly gray to gray-brown hood, back, and sides.

Adult female (above) paler overall than male, with gray hood. Common breeder over much of the state, and juveniles (below) are quite conspicuous in summer, a source of confusion for beginning birders. Juvenile sparrow-like, with unmarked head. White outer tail feathers obvious when feeding or flying.

Yellow-breasted Chat

Icteria virens

L 7.5" | **WS** 10"

Noisy Yellow-breasted Chats are breeding birds of shrubby riparian woodland from the lower east slopes of the Cascades east. Most arrive in May and leave in August; they are only rarely seen in migration. These are birds of dense underbrush, hopping around with tail cocked like a large, yellow-breasted wren. Large and colorful as they are, chats are surprisingly difficult to see. The best opportunity is when a male ascends a tree to sing, or floats with slow wingbeats over a clearing in "butterfly flight" while in full song. The song is a continuous mixture of varied whistles, chatters, and chuckles, often persisting into the night.

Tanager-sized, with fairly heavy bill; much larger than warblers. Long tail often cocked. Olive or greenish above. Head with white eyebrow and malar stripe. Breast bright yellow-orange, belly white.

Yellow-headed Blackbird

Xanthocephalus xanthocephalus

L 9-10" | **WS** 16-18"

This big, bright blackbird is a common breeding species of cattail and bulrush marshes east of the Cascades. Ridgefield NWR and a few other locations on the westside also have breeding colonies. Males arrive in April and displace Red-winged Blackbirds from the best territories, then attempt to attract as many females as possible. Adults feed their chicks on dragonflies and damselflies. Most leave the state in winter, but a few are found in mixed blackbird flocks at cattle feedlots, especially in the southern part of the Columbia Basin. The song is a combination of musical notes and an ear-rending nasal snarl, accompanied by spectacular displays. Calls are *chuck* notes, deeper than those of other blackbirds.

Large blackbird. Male with yellow head and breast; large white patches at wrist, best seen in flight or in courtship display. Look for the tiny circle of yellow feathers around the vent. Female (below) much smaller than male; brown, with dull yellowish face, throat, and breast. Juvenile brown, with ochre head and breast.

Bobolink

Dolichonyx oryzivorus

L 6-8" | **WS** 10-11.5"

Extremely long-distance migrants, Bobolinks arrive in Washington in May from wintering grounds south of the Equator. They leave us in August after breeding in hay meadows in valleys in the four northeastern counties, for example, at Aeneas Creek, Curlew Lake, and Cusick. The species is otherwise a very rare migrant anywhere in the state. The seasonal plumage change is dramatic, with fall females and fall males both yellowish brown sparrow-like birds. The song is a sprightly series of tinkling notes, often given in display flight, the call a characteristic *pink*.

Small blackbird with finchlike bill. Breeding-plumaged male (left) black, with large white and golden patches above. Larger than any similar sparrow; note pointed tail feathers. Female (below) and nonbreeding male entirely washed buffy below, finely streaked on sides. Strong black crown stripes, vivid buffy eyebrow with faint dark stripe behind eye.

Western Meadowlark

Sturnella neglecta

L 9.5" | **WS** 14.5"

Meadowlarks breed throughout open areas east of the Cascades, including sagebrush flats, grassland, and cropland. Most birds leave in winter, but small numbers remain, especially in the southern Columbia Basin. Very few breed on the westside, where many more are seen in winter on farmlands and meadows, presumably migrants from the interior. Meadowlarks nest and feed on the ground, their brown, streaked upperparts camouflaging them perfectly, but in spring they fly up to fence posts and utility wires to sing. Even in silhouette, they are easily distinguished by their long legs and short tail. Their song, so evocative of open spaces, consists of two pure whistles followed by a slurred multi-note phrase. Call is a rapid chatter.

Long-billed, short-tailed. Entirely streaked and barred with brown and black above. Bright yellow eyebrow, throat, and underparts, with vivid black V on breast. White outer tail feathers conspicuous in flight.

Bullock's Oriole

Icterus bullockii

L 9" | **WS** 12"

Bullock's Orioles breed widely in the state May–August. They are more common east, where there are more of the riparian corridors and groves that they prefer, and are as common around human habitations as anywhere. They often wander away from the trees to feed well out in sagebrush and other shrubs. On the westside, they are usually found in cottonwoods in the Puget Trough and along the Columbia River. The finely woven hanging nest persists into winter. The song begins with chucks and proceeds through rapid musical notes to end in an upslurred *wheet*. Call is a rapid chatter.

Adult male bright orange and black, with large white wing patches. Note eyebrow and eye line. Tail with large orange patches conspicuous in flight. Female (left) mostly gray-brown, with dull orange or yellow-orange on head, breast, and tail. Conspicuous white wingbars. Thin bill unlike a tanager's.

Tricolored Blackbird

Agelaius tricolor

L 9" | **WS** 14"

Tricolored Blackbirds were first found in Washington along Wilson Creek in 1998, and several additional breeding sites have been discovered since. Most birds are seen in marshes between Othello and Columbia NWR to the northwest, including a few in winter flocks. They breed in dense colonies, with smaller individual territories than those of Red-winged Blackbirds. Beware the possibility of confusion with a Red-winged Blackbird with a faded golden border to the epaulet. The song is similar to that of the Red-winged, but harsher and more nasal. The chorus of many voices in a colony is discordant.

Male shiny black with dark crimson-red epaulets bordered white to cream, the two colors contrasting strongly.

Female dark brown with pale eyebrow and streaked breast, sharply pointed bill.

Red-winged Blackbird
Agelaius phoeniceus

L 9" | **WS** 13"

This familiar bird is resident throughout the state, even in cities. It breeds in wetlands of all kinds, from extensive marshes to cattail-fringed lakes, roadside ditches, and wet subalpine meadows. Flocks of Red-winged Blackbirds leave the marshes in winter to visit feeders, croplands, dairy farms, and feedlots, wherever seeds are available. The sexes are often segregated in winter, with flocks of males tending to winter farther north than females. Adult males often breed with multiple females; one-year-old males try to do the same but usually fail. The song is the familiar *o-ka-leeeee*, one of the first sounds of spring, and the calls are *chack* notes.

Male black, with bright red-orange wing patch bordered by buffy-orange line, forming "epaulets" that can be mostly hidden when not being displayed.

First-year male with subdued epaulet. Many wing feathers with narrow pale edges.

Female smaller than male, heavily streaked all over. Differs from sparrows in larger size, more slender bill, darker plumage, and evenly and heavily streaked underparts. Some have hint of red epaulets or reddish throat.

Brown-headed Cowbird

Molothrus ater

L 7.5" | **WS** 12"

Cowbirds occur statewide April–August, breeding in open and semiopen habitats. Females lay their eggs in the nests of other birds, and those foster parents then raise the young cowbirds. Most cowbirds depart to the south in winter, but small flocks winter with other blackbirds near large-scale sources of food such as cattle feedlots. The male's song is a couple of liquid notes and a high-pitched squeak, usually accompanied by a puffed-up display. Females have a loud chattering call.

Juvenile like female but paler, with all feathers of back and wings pale-fringed. Underparts vaguely streaked and mottled. 'The streaked juveniles, never with cowbird parents, present an identification challenge in late summer.

Small blackbird with finchlike bill. Male entirely shiny black with brown head. First-year males have browner primaries.

Female uniform brown, with black conical bill. No other bird its size is as plain.

Brewer's Blackbird

Euphagus cyanocephalus

L 9" | **WS** 15.5"

This open-country blackbird occurs over most of the state at low elevations, requiring a mixture of open areas for feeding and shrubs for nesting. Resident on the westside, it is present only April–September in more northerly areas east of the Cascades. It is common in towns and farmland as well as in shrub steppe and at riparian edges. In larger cities, look for them at shopping centers with rows of shrubs for nesting. Their flight is steadier than that of a Red-winged Blackbird, with no undulations, and the tail is longer. The typical song is a guttural note rising into a grating squeak.

Slender bill and fairly long tail. Male iridescent bluish- or greenish-black, with purple head; eyes yellow. Female (below) light to medium brown; eyes dark.

Northern Waterthrush

Parkesia noveboracensis

L 6" | **WS** 9.5"

Northern Waterthrushes breed widely in the wild northeastern corner of the state, from eastern Okanogan County east. They are birds of wetlands, breeding around lakes and bogs and along streams, and preferring to forage on logs, rocks, and mud banks at the water's edge. Present May–August, they have also been seen in migration elsewhere in the state, even in the western lowlands, where a few birds have wintered. Like several other species of waterside birds, waterthrushes bob the rear end up and down. The song begins with a series of sweet notes, then accelerates into a lower-pitched series of *chu chu chu chu chu*. The call is a loud *chink*.

Dark brown above, with vivid white eyebrow. Pale buffy to almost white below, with entire underparts heavily streaked. Bobs rear end of body up and down.

Orange-crowned Warbler

Leiothlypis celata

L 5" | **WS** 7"

This wide-ranging bird arrives in Washington in mid–April, and is a common breeder in low mixed woodland with good shrub cover in the western lowlands; it also breeds sparsely on the east slope of the Cascades, and more commonly in the Northeastern Highlands and Blue Mountains. Grayer birds from Alaska and boreal Canada migrate through the state in good numbers spring and fall. All are gone by October. Orange-crowns generally remain in dense vegetation, and seeing the concealed orange crown is a challenge. The song is a weak trill, trailing off at the end. The call is a sharp *chip*.

Entirely greenish to yellowish, with faint paler eyebrow and hint of a broken eye ring. Westside breeding birds are very yellow below. Northern birds (left), common in migration, are gray to dull greenish.

Nashville Warbler

Leiothlypis ruficapilla

L 5" **WS** 7.5"

Nashville Warblers breed east of the Cascades crest, where they are present from late April into September in dry woodland with many small trees and shrubs. They are also rare breeders and uncommon migrants west. Like most warblers, Nashvilles forage very actively, often at the tips of branches, and they take very small insects with their petite bills. Watch for the usually hidden rufous crown patch of a displaying male. Usually in dense vegetation, they are most easily found by listening for the two-part song, a series of abrupt single notes followed by a trill. Call is a metallic *chip*.

Olive back, wings, and tail; gray head with white eye ring and concealed chestnut crown patch. Yellow underparts with small whitish patch at vent.

MacGillivray's Warbler

Geothlypis tolmiei

L 5" | **WS** 7.5"

This is the most skulking of our breeding warblers, difficult to see well until a male flies up to a higher perch to sing. MacGillivray's Warblers are present late April through early September, breeding throughout the state in riparian vegetation with dense shrubs. In the western lowlands, they are particularly common in revegetating clearcuts and other second-growth shrublands. The song is a strong series of single or double notes, the call a typical warbler *chip*.

Gray head. Thick, incomplete eye ring distinctive. Male's upper breast smudged black.

Female lacks black on breast.

Common Yellowthroat

Geothlypis trichas

L 5" | **WS** 7"

Common Yellowthroats are one of North America's most widespread warblers. These shy wetland birds are at home in marshes large and small, on willow-bordered lake shores, and in sphagnum bogs from April through the summer. Migrants are infrequently seen away from these habitats; all are gone by late October. The black-masked males ascend marsh vegetation to sing their persistent *chewee-chewee-chewee-chu*, or *wichity-wichity-wichity*. The call is a low *chuck*.

Olive above and on sides, with bright yellow throat. Male's extensive black mask bordered by white above.

Olive sides a good distinction from other warblers with yellow underparts. Female lacks black-and-white head markings.

American Redstart

Setophaga ruticilla

L 5" | **WS** 8"

These very distinctive warblers flit and flutter with tail spread, twitching it back and forth to scare up insects that they capture in flight. Present May–September, redstarts breed in broadleaf forests with cottonwoods, alders, aspens, willows, and birches in the Northeast Highlands. A few breeding pairs are scattered along the east slope of the Cascades south to Kittitas County, and even smaller numbers are found in river valleys on the westside. Both the song and the call are similar to those of the Yellow Warbler, but the song is a bit higher-pitched and thinner and often includes doubled notes.

Very active warbler with short bill, flicking wings, and flared tail. Male black above and on upper breast; white belly. Orange breast sides, orange wing and tail patches.

Tail swings back and forth while foraging, displaying colorful patches. Female gray and olive, with yellow breast, wing, and tail patches. First-year male similar, but with black markings on head and breast.

Yellow Warbler

Setophaga petechia

L 5" | **WS** 8"

This is a common breeder throughout the state, present May–September in willows, cottonwoods, and alders near water. Common to the north in Alaska and all across Canada, many birds also migrate through the state spring and fall. Among numerous other land-based migrants, Yellow Warblers have been seen more than once approaching boats far off Westport from late August to late September. The two-part song of high notes is often written as *sweet sweet sweet I'm so sweet*. The call is a *chip* note, richer than that of many other warblers.

Yellow all over, with greener back, wings, and tail. Broad yellow edgings on wing feathers, yellow patches in tail. Male's bright yellow underparts with chestnut stripes.

Only yellow warbler with unmarked face and yellow tail patches. Female paler yellow than male, sometimes with faint chestnut stripes below.

Yellow-rumped Warbler

Setophaga coronata

L 5.5" | **WS** 9"

Two distinguishable populations of Yellow-rumped Warblers occur in Washington. The Audubon's race, with a yellow throat, breeds late April to September throughout the state in dry and wet conifer forests, most commonly in the mountains. Abundant as a migrant everywhere, it also winters in small numbers. The northerly Myrtle race, with a white throat, is a bit less common as a migrant, but winters more commonly west. Yellow-rumped Warblers of all populations take insects from the air in the warmer seasons, then turn to eating fruit in the winter, including wax myrtles near the coast and unpicked apples east. They also regularly visit feeders for suet. The song is a high-pitched series of notes a bit slower than a trill. The calls differ between populations: Audubon's gives a metallic *tip*, Myrtle a drier *tup*.

Gray, black, and white, with yellow patches on crown, rump, and sides of breast. Audubon's Yellow-rumped with white eye ring and yellow throat. Male in breeding plumage has white wing patches.

Female Audubon's resembles male, but lacks extensive solid gray to black on breast.

Breeding male Myrtle with yellow crown, rump, and breast patches, but throat white; dark cheek bordered by short white eyebrow.

Nonbreeding Yellow-rumpeds are plain, streaked warblers with sometimes inconspicuous yellow patches on crown, rump, and breast. Even in winter, white eyebrow and throat indicate Myrtle; Audubon's has eye ring and yellow throat, sometimes very pale.

Black-throated Gray Warbler

Setophaga nigrescens

L 5" | **WS** 8"

These slightly chickadee-like warblers, with black cheeks and a tiny yellow spot before the eye, occur mid-April through September in deciduous and mixed woodlands throughout the western lowlands, and more locally on the lower east slope of the Cascades from Kittitas County south. They shun the dense conifer forest favored by Townsend's Warblers. Usually high in the trees while breeding, they vary their foraging height more during migration. The song is a series of buzzy notes, the last higher, *zoo zoo zoo zeee*; the call is a sharp *chip*.

Gray above and white below, with wide white wingbars. Black-and-white-striped head, streaked sides. Yellow spot in front of eye. Male has black throat.

Female and immature have white or speckled throat.

Townsend's Warbler

Setophaga townsendi

L 5" | **WS** 8"

These active and brightly colored warblers are common from late April to early September in montane and lowland wet conifer forests throughout Washington. They feed on small insects, including spruce budworms, high in the trees, where they also nest. They are common everywhere in migration, but most leave the state in winter. Small numbers remain in the Puget Sound lowlands, where they switch in large part to urban and suburban suet feeders. Watch them use the same hovering skills they use to capture leaf-dwelling insects. The song is a series of high-pitched whistles, the last notes buzzier. The call is a sharp *chip*.

Olive back, yellow face and breast; white wingbars and prominently dark-streaked flanks. Male with black face patch and throat.

Female and immature have paler face patch, yellow throat.

Hermit Warbler

Setophaga occidentalis

L 5" | **WS** 8"

This yellow-headed warbler breeds May–August from the east side of the Olympics and southern King County south, occupying wet conifer forest from near sea level to the subalpine zone. Capitol Forest is a particularly good site. Hermits hybridize with Townsend's Warblers throughout much of their range in Washington, and in some areas in the South Cascades, hybrids are as common as either parent species; hybrids have been detected almost to the Canadian border. Townsend's Warblers apparently outcompete Hermits, and may be replacing them entirely in some areas. The songs and calls of Hermit Warblers and hybrids are much like those of Townsend's.

Gray back with fine streaks, prominent white wingbars. Male (above) with yellow head, black throat, and some black on hind crown. Unmarked white underparts. Any yellow or streaks on underparts or greenish on back indicate hybridization with Townsend's. Female (left) with dusky cheeks, fine streaks on side, and less or no black on throat.

Wilson's Warbler

Cardellina pusilla

L 5" **WS** 7"

These black-capped warblers often move about the under-
growth with their tail cocked and twitching like a wren. They
breed widely in the wet forests of the state May–September, and
are also among the most common migrants throughout, even in
isolated copses in the Columbia Basin. During migration waves
in spring and fall in Seattle, these little yellow birds seem to
be in every wooded yard. Some females of the westside population have black caps like males. The song is a series of even *chip*
notes; the metallic *chip* call sounds like half of the double note
of a Pacific Wren, a bird that shares its habitat.

Small and bright yellow,
a bit darker above.
Relatively long tail, often
twitched. Dark eye on
unmarked face. Male
with shiny black cap.

Some females in
western lowlands are
like males in plumage.
Others, especially east
of the Cascades, have
black cap replaced by
olive-yellow.

Western Tanager

Piranga ludoviciana

L 7" | **WS** 11.5"

Western Tanagers bring a flash of tropical color to the woodlands of the state. Watch them capturing insects on the foliage and sallying out to catch them in flight. Tanagers are present May to mid-September, breeding throughout conifer and mixed forests, especially favoring Douglas-fir, from the lowlands almost to the subalpine. They are common migrants everywhere, sometimes half a dozen in the same tree. The song is robin-like, but with a strong burry element, likened to a robin with a cold. The call is a staccato but musical *perdick*, perhaps more easily remembered as *pretty*.

Adult male black and yellow, with bright red head and sometimes upper breast. First-year male with brownish primaries, usually much less red on head.

Female olive and yellow, with prominent yellow to white wingbars. Individuals vary from gray to entirely yellow below.

Black-headed Grosbeak

Pheucticus melanocephalus

L 8" | **WS** 12.5"

These brightly marked, big-billed birds are visitors May–
September in low-elevation deciduous forests and riparian
strips throughout the state, strongly associated with alders,
willows, maples, cottonwoods, and aspens. They are not as
conspicuous in migration as Western Tanagers and some of the
warblers, presumably because few grosbeaks breed much to
our north. They search for fruits and insects at mid-levels and
in the canopy. The song is a series of rich warbled notes, like
"a robin on helium"; each song is followed by a pause, unlike
the similar robin song that can go on and on. The call is a loud,
sharp *pik*.

Bill thick and pale. Wings with showy
white wingbars and spots. Adult male's
head, back, wings, and tail mostly black.
Underparts and rump orange, darker
than orioles. First-year male similar, but
duller, with brown primaries.

Female brown above, with prominent
white wingbars, supercilium, and malar
stripe. Orange below, brightest on
breast, with fine streaks on sides.

Lazuli Bunting
Passerina amoena

L 5.5" **WS** 9"

Lazuli Buntings breed widely May–August from the Cascades crest east, most commonly on shrubby hillsides and canyon slopes, but also in riparian strips and open woodland with much shrub cover. They are also very local breeders in more open areas of the Puget Trough. Few are seen in migration elsewhere. They forage in shrubs for fruits and on the ground for seeds; they also take insects from foliage or even from the air. They sing persistently, even in the heat of the day, a series of paired high-pitched whistled notes, each pair at a different pitch, for example, *chew chew wheet wheet chip chip*. Common calls include a sharp *tip* and short *buzz*.

Prominent white or buffy wingbars and sparrow-like bill distinguish all Lazuli Buntings from Western Bluebirds. Adult male sky-blue above, including wings and tail. Rusty breast patch, white lower breast and belly. Female (left) plain light brown. Wings may be tinged blue. Two white or buffy wingbars. Sparrowlike, but lack of streaking distinctive.

Acknowledgments

I wish to thank Andy Stepniewski and Netta Smith for their careful reading of the manuscript. Andy, with his great knowledge of birds of the state, upgraded the information about status and had many good suggestions, while both were good at catching writing errors. Thanks to Andy and Ryan Merrill for helping me navigate around eBird, and thanks to all the Washington tweeters for responding to individual questions. I am very grateful to Seattle Audubon Society for setting up the Master Birders program three decades ago and for the 300 students who have participated in the program and who have enlightened me as much as I hope I enlightened them. Again I want to thank Netta Smith for being such a wonderful companion for all these years and all those birds.

This book has been a pleasure to write, allowing me to share my knowledge of Washington birds with many more people, and I thank George Scott for asking me to write the book and for doing such a fine job of producing it.

Scott & Nix Acknowledgments

Many thanks to Jeffrey A. Gordon and Liz Gordon, Ted Floyd, and everyone at the American Birding Association for their good work. Thanks to Alan Poole, Miyoko Chu, and especially Kevin J. McGowan at the Cornell Lab of Ornithology for their bird measurement data sets. We give special thanks to Brian E. Small, and all the other contributors for their extraordinary photographs in the guide. We thank Rick Wright for his work on the manuscript; James Montalbano of Terminal Design for his typefaces; Charles Nix for the series design; and René Nedelkoff and Nancy Wakeland of Porter Print Group for shepherding this book through print production.

Image Credits

(T) = Top, (B) = Bottom, (L) = Left, (R) = Right; pages with multiple images from one source are indicated by a single credit.

XIII–XXX Brian E. Small. 2–6 Brian E. Small. 7 Brian E. Small (T), Dennis Paulson(B). 8–14 Brian E. Small. 15 Brian E. Small (T), Gregg Thompson (B). 16–40 Brian E. Small. 41 Bob Steele. 42 Alan Murphy (T), Brian E. Small (B). 43–44 Brian E. Small. 45 Wendy Duncan (L), Robert Pearson (R). 46–47 Brian E. Small. 48 Gregg Thompson (L), Brian E. Small (R). 49 Brian E. Small. 50 Brian E. Small (T), Gregg Thompson (B). 51–53 Brian E. Small. 54 Brian E. Small (T), Joe Fuhrman (B). 55–63 Brian E. Small. 64 Mike Danzenbaker. 65 Bob Steele. 66–79 Brian E. Small. 80 Brian E. Small (T), Gregg Thompson (B). 81–110 Brian E. Small. 111 Brian E. Small (T), Bob Steele (B). 112 Alan Murphy. 113 Brian E. Small (T), Mike Danzenbaker (B). 114 Brian E. Small. 115 Gregg Thompson (T), Alan Murphy (B). 116 Alan Murphy. 117 Glenn Bartley (T), Gregg Thompson (B). 118 Brian E. Small. 119 Mike Danzenbaker. 120 Glenn Bartley (T), Brian E. Small (B). 121 Gregg Thompson. 122–126 Brian E. Small. 127 Brian E. Small (T), Dennis Paulson (B). 128 Dennis Paulson (T), Brian E. Small (B). 129 Brian E. Small. 130 Jacob Spendelow. 131 Dennis Paulson (T), Brian E. Small (B). 132 Alan Murphy. 133 Dennis Paulson. 134–140 Brian E. Small. 141 Brian E. Small (T), Alan Murphy (B). 142 Dennis Paulson. 143 Alan Murphy. 144–145 Mike Danzenbaker. 146 Joe Fuhrman (T), Brian E. Small (B). 147 Brian E. Small (T), Dennis Paulson (B). 148–160 Brian E. Small. 161 Gregg Thompson. 162–166 Brian E. Small. 167 Netta Smith (T), Alan Murphy (B). 168–169 Brian E. Small. 170 Gregg Thompson. 171–176 Brian E. Small. 177 Gregg Thompson. 178–183 Brian E. Small. 184 Jacob Spendelow. 185–193 Brian E. Small. 194 Dennis Paulson (L), Brian E. Small (R). 195 Brian E. Small (L), Gregg Thompson (R). 196–199 Brian E. Small. 200 Brian E. Small (T), Gregg Thompson (B). 201 Brian E. Small. 202 Brian E. Small (T), Joe Fuhrman (B). 203–225 Brian E. Small. 226 Brian E. Small (T), Dennis Paulson (B). 227–242 Brian E. Small. 243 Gregg Thompson. 244–255 Brian E. Small. 256–257 Gregg Thompson. 258–262 Brian E. Small. 263 Brian E. Small (T), Dennis Paulson (B). 264–271 Brian E. Small. 272 Garth McElroy. 273–275 Brian E. Small. 276 Alan Murphy. 277–279 Brian E. Small. 280 Brian E. Small (T), Jim Zipp (B). 281 Gregg Thompson. 282–283 Brian E. Small. 284 Jacob Spendelow. 285–291 Brian E. Small. 292 Dennis Paulson (T), Brian E. Small (B). 293–295 Brian E. Small. 296 Netta Smith. 297–326 Brian E. Small.

Official Washington Ornithological Society Checklist of Washington Birds

This list includes all 518 bird species that have been reported in Washington State as of April 2020, except for four species that have not been seen in the last fifty years. Asterisked species are review species, observations of which (as well as species not on the list) should be submitted to the Washington Bird Records Committee (wbrc@wos.org). The checklist follows the nomenclature and taxonomic sequence of the American Ornithological Society's *Check-list of North American Birds*, through the 61st Supplement (2020).

Anatidae: Waterfowl

☐ Fulvous Whistling-Duck*
☐ Emperor Goose
☐ Snow Goose
☐ Ross's Goose
☐ Greater White-fronted Goose
☐ Taiga Bean-Goose*
☐ Brant
☐ Cackling Goose
☐ Canada Goose
☐ Trumpeter Swan
☐ Tundra Swan
☐ Whooper Swan*
☐ Wood Duck
☐ Baikal Teal*
☐ Garganey*
☐ Blue-winged Teal
☐ Cinnamon Teal
☐ Northern Shoveler
☐ Gadwall
☐ Falcated Duck*
☐ Eurasian Wigeon

☐ American Wigeon
☐ Mallard
☐ Northern Pintail
☐ Green-winged Teal
☐ Canvasback
☐ Redhead
☐ Ring-necked Duck
☐ Tufted Duck
☐ Greater Scaup
☐ Lesser Scaup
☐ Steller's Eider*
☐ King Eider*
☐ Common Eider*
☐ Harlequin Duck
☐ Surf Scoter
☐ White-winged Scoter
☐ Black Scoter
☐ Long-tailed Duck
☐ Bufflehead
☐ Common Goldeneye
☐ Barrow's Goldeneye
☐ Smew*

☐ Hooded Merganser
☐ Common Merganser
☐ Red-breasted Merganser
☐ Ruddy Duck

Odontophoridae: New World Quails

☐ Mountain Quail
☐ Northern Bobwhite
☐ California Quail

Phasianidae: Partridges, Grouse & Turkeys

☐ Chukar
☐ Gray Partridge
☐ Ring-necked Pheasant
☐ Ruffed Grouse
☐ Greater Sage-Grouse
☐ Spruce Grouse
☐ White-tailed Ptarmigan
☐ Dusky Grouse
☐ Sooty Grouse
☐ Sharp-tailed Grouse
☐ Wild Turkey

Podicipedidae: Grebes

☐ Pied-billed Grebe
☐ Horned Grebe
☐ Red-necked Grebe
☐ Eared Grebe
☐ Western Grebe
☐ Clark's Grebe

Columbidae: Pigeon & Doves

☐ Rock Pigeon
☐ Band-tailed Pigeon
☐ Eurasian Collared-Dove
☐ White-winged Dove*
☐ Mourning Dove

Cuculidae: Cuckoos

☐ Yellow-billed Cuckoo*
☐ Black-billed Cuckoo*

Caprimulgidae: Nightjars

☐ Common Nighthawk
☐ Common Poorwill

Apodidae: Swifts

☐ Black Swift
☐ Vaux's Swift
☐ White-throated Swift

Trochilidae: Hummingbirds

☐ Ruby-throated Hummingbird*
☐ Black-chinned Hummingbird
☐ Anna's Hummingbird
☐ Costa's Hummingbird*
☐ Broad-tailed Hummingbird*
☐ Rufous Hummingbird
☐ Calliope Hummingbird
☐ Broad-billed Hummingbird*

Rallidae: Rails

☐ Yellow Rail*
☐ Virginia Rail
☐ Sora
☐ Purple Gallinule*
☐ American Coot

Gruidae: Cranes

☐ Sandhill Crane

Recurvirostridae: Stilts & Avocets

☐ Black-necked Stilt
☐ American Avocet

Haematopodidae: Oystercatchers

☐ Black Oystercatcher

Charadriidae: Plovers

☐ Black-bellied Plover
☐ American Golden-Plover
☐ Pacific Golden-Plover
☐ Eurasian Dotterel*
☐ Killdeer
☐ Common Ringed-Plover*
☐ Semipalmated Plover
☐ Piping Plover*
☐ Lesser Sand-Plover*
☐ Wilson's Plover*
☐ Mountain Plover*
☐ Snowy Plover

Scolopacidae: Sandpipers

☐ Upland Sandpiper*
☐ Bristle-thighed Curlew*
☐ Whimbrel
☐ Long-billed Curlew
☐ Bar-tailed Godwit
☐ Hudsonian Godwit
☐ Marbled Godwit
☐ Ruddy Turnstone
☐ Black Turnstone
☐ Red Knot
☐ Surfbird
☐ Ruff
☐ Sharp-tailed Sandpiper
☐ Stilt Sandpiper
☐ Curlew Sandpiper*
☐ Temminck's Stint*
☐ Red-necked Stint*
☐ Sanderling
☐ Dunlin
☐ Rock Sandpiper
☐ Baird's Sandpiper
☐ Little Stint*
☐ Least Sandpiper
☐ White-rumped Sandpiper*

☐ Buff-breasted Sandpiper
☐ Pectoral Sandpiper
☐ Semipalmated Sandpiper
☐ Western Sandpiper
☐ Short-billed Dowitcher
☐ Long-billed Dowitcher
☐ Jack Snipe*
☐ Wilson's Snipe
☐ Spotted Sandpiper
☐ Solitary Sandpiper
☐ Gray-tailed Tattler*
☐ Wandering Tattler
☐ Lesser Yellowlegs
☐ Willet
☐ Spotted Redshank*
☐ Greater Yellowlegs
☐ Wood Sandpiper*
☐ Wilson's Phalarope
☐ Red-necked Phalarope
☐ Red Phalarope

Stercorariidae: Jaegers & Skuas

☐ South Polar Skua
☐ Pomarine Jaeger
☐ Parasitic Jaeger
☐ Long-tailed Jaeger

Alcidae: Auks, Murres & Puffins

☐ Common Murre
☐ Thick-billed Murre*
☐ Pigeon Guillemot
☐ Long-billed Murrelet*
☐ Marbled Murrelet
☐ Kittlitz's Murrelet*
☐ Scripps's Murrelet
☐ Guadalupe Murrelet*
☐ Ancient Murrelet
☐ Cassin's Auklet
☐ Parakeet Auklet

- ☐ Least Auklet*
- ☐ Crested Auklet*
- ☐ Rhinoceros Auklet
- ☐ Horned Puffin
- ☐ Tufted Puffin

Laridae: Gulls, Terns & Skimmers

- ☐ Swallow-tailed Gull*
- ☐ Black-legged Kittiwake
- ☐ Red-legged Kittiwake*
- ☐ Ivory Gull*
- ☐ Sabine's Gull
- ☐ Bonaparte's Gull
- ☐ Black-headed Gull*
- ☐ Little Gull*
- ☐ Ross's Gull*
- ☐ Laughing Gull*
- ☐ Franklin's Gull
- ☐ Black-tailed Gull*
- ☐ Heermann's Gull
- ☐ Mew Gull
- ☐ Ring-billed Gull
- ☐ Western Gull
- ☐ California Gull
- ☐ Herring Gull
- ☐ Iceland Gull
- ☐ Lesser Black-backed Gull
- ☐ Slaty-backed Gull*
- ☐ Glaucous-winged Gull
- ☐ Glaucous Gull
- ☐ Great Black-backed Gull*
- ☐ Least Tern*
- ☐ Caspian Tern
- ☐ Black Tern
- ☐ Common Tern
- ☐ Arctic Tern
- ☐ Forster's Tern
- ☐ Elegant Tern

Gaviidae: Loons

- ☐ Red-throated Loon
- ☐ Arctic Loon*
- ☐ Pacific Loon
- ☐ Common Loon
- ☐ Yellow-billed Loon

Diomedeidae: Albatrosses

- ☐ White-capped Albatross*
- ☐ Laysan Albatross
- ☐ Black-footed Albatross
- ☐ Short-tailed Albatross

Oceanitidae: Southern Storm-Petrels

- ☐ Wilson's Storm-Petrel*

Hydrobatidae: Northern Storm-Petrels

- ☐ Fork-tailed Storm Petrel
- ☐ Leach's Storm Petrel
- ☐ Ashy Storm-Petrel*

Procellariidae: Petrels

- ☐ Northern Fulmar
- ☐ Providence Petrel*
- ☐ Murphy's Petrel
- ☐ Mottled Petrel
- ☐ Hawaiian Petrel*
- ☐ Cook's Petrel*
- ☐ Wedge-tailed Shearwater*
- ☐ Buller's Shearwater
- ☐ Short-tailed Shearwater
- ☐ Sooty Shearwater
- ☐ Great Shearwater*
- ☐ Pink-footed Shearwater
- ☐ Flesh-footed Shearwater
- ☐ Manx Shearwater

Fregatidae: Frigatebirds

☐ Magnificent Frigatebird*

Sulidae: Boobies & Gannets

☐ Blue-footed Booby*
☐ Brown Booby
☐ Red-footed Booby*

Phalacrocoracidae: Cormorants

☐ Brandt's Cormorant
☐ Double-crested Cormorant
☐ Pelagic Cormorant

Pelecanidae: Pelicans

☐ American White Pelican
☐ Brown Pelican

Ardeidae: Herons & Bitterns

☐ American Bittern
☐ Great Blue Heron
☐ Great Egret
☐ Snowy Egret*
☐ Little Blue Heron*
☐ Cattle Egret*
☐ Green Heron
☐ Black-crowned Night-Heron
☐ Yellow-crowned Night-Heron*

Threskiornithidae: Ibises & Spoonbills

☐ White Ibis*
☐ Glossy Ibis*
☐ White-faced Ibis

Cathartidae: New World Vultures

☐ Turkey Vulture

Pandionidae: Ospreys

☐ Osprey

Accipitridae: Hawks & Eagles

☐ White-tailed Kite
☐ Golden Eagle
☐ Northern Harrier
☐ Sharp-shinned Hawk
☐ Cooper's Hawk
☐ Northern Goshawk
☐ Bald Eagle
☐ Red-shouldered Hawk
☐ Broad-winged Hawk
☐ Swainson's Hawk
☐ Zone-tailed Hawk*
☐ Red-tailed Hawk
☐ Rough-legged Hawk
☐ Ferruginous Hawk

Tytonidae: Barn Owls

☐ Barn Owl

Strigidae: True Owls

☐ Flammulated Owl
☐ Western Screech-Owl
☐ Great Horned Owl
☐ Snowy Owl
☐ Northern Hawk Owl
☐ Northern Pygmy-Owl
☐ Burrowing Owl
☐ Spotted Owl
☐ Barred Owl
☐ Great Gray Owl
☐ Long-eared Owl
☐ Short-eared Owl
☐ Boreal Owl
☐ Northern Saw-whet Owl

Alcedinidae: Kingfishers

☐ Belted Kingfisher

Picidae: Woodpeckers

☐ Lewis's Woodpecker
☐ Acorn Woodpecker
☐ Williamson's Sapsucker
☐ Yellow-bellied Sapsucker*
☐ Red-naped Sapsucker
☐ Red-breasted Sapsucker
☐ American Three-toed Woodpecker
☐ Black-backed Woodpecker
☐ Downy Woodpecker
☐ Hairy Woodpecker
☐ White-headed Woodpecker
☐ Northern Flicker
☐ Pileated Woodpecker

Falconidae: Falcons

☐ Crested Caracara*
☐ American Kestrel
☐ Merlin
☐ Eurasian Hobby*
☐ Gyrfalcon
☐ Peregrine Falcon
☐ Prairie Falcon

Tyrannidae: Tyrant Flycatchers

☐ Dusky-capped Flycatcher*
☐ Ash-throated Flycatcher
☐ Variegated Flycatcher*
☐ Tropical Kingbird
☐ Western Kingbird
☐ Eastern Kingbird
☐ Scissor-tailed Flycatcher*
☐ Fork-tailed Flycatcher*
☐ Olive-sided Flycatcher
☐ Greater Pewee*
☐ Western Wood-Pewee
☐ Eastern Wood-Pewee*

☐ Yellow-bellied Flycatcher*
☐ Alder Flycatcher*
☐ Willow Flycatcher
☐ Least Flycatcher
☐ Hammond's Flycatcher
☐ Gray Flycatcher
☐ Dusky Flycatcher
☐ Pacific-slope Flycatcher
☐ Black Phoebe
☐ Eastern Phoebe*
☐ Say's Phoebe
☐ Vermilion Flycatcher*

Laniidae: Shrikes

☐ Loggerhead Shrike
☐ Northern Shrike

Vireonidae: Vireos

☐ White-eyed Vireo*
☐ Bell's Vireo*
☐ Hutton's Vireo
☐ Yellow-throated Vireo*
☐ Cassin's Vireo
☐ Blue-headed Vireo*
☐ Philadelphia Vireo*
☐ Warbling Vireo
☐ Red-eyed Vireo

Corvidae: Crows and Jays

☐ Canada Jay
☐ Steller's Jay
☐ Blue Jay
☐ California Scrub-Jay
☐ Woodhouse's Scrub-Jay*
☐ Clark's Nutcracker
☐ Black-billed Magpie
☐ American Crow
☐ Common Raven

Alaudidae: Larks

☐ Eurasian Skylark*
☐ Horned Lark

Hirundinidae: Swallows

☐ Bank Swallow
☐ Tree Swallow
☐ Violet-green Swallow
☐ N. Rough-winged Swallow
☐ Purple Martin
☐ Barn Swallow
☐ Cliff Swallow

Paridae: Chickadees & Titmice

☐ Black-capped Chickadee
☐ Mountain Chickadee
☐ Chestnut-backed Chickadee
☐ Boreal Chickadee

Aegithalidae: Long-tailed Tits

☐ Bushtit

Sittidae: Nuthatches

☐ Red-breasted Nuthatch
☐ White-breasted Nuthatch
☐ Pygmy Nuthatch

Certhiidae: Creepers

☐ Brown Creeper

Troglodytidae: Wrens

☐ Rock Wren
☐ Canyon Wren
☐ House Wren
☐ Pacific Wren
☐ Marsh Wren
☐ Bewick's Wren

Polioptilidae: Gnatcatchers

☐ Blue-gray Gnatcatcher*

Cinclidae: Dippers

☐ American Dipper

Regulidae: Kinglets

☐ Golden-crowned Kinglet
☐ Ruby-crowned Kinglet

Turdidae: Thrushes

☐ Red-fanked Bluetail*
☐ Northern Wheatear*
☐ Western Bluebird
☐ Mountain Bluebird
☐ Townsend's Solitaire
☐ Veery
☐ Swainson's Thrush
☐ Hermit Thrush
☐ Dusky Thrush*
☐ Redwing*
☐ American Robin
☐ Varied Thrush

Mimidae: Catbirds, Mockingbirds and Thrashers

☐ Gray Catbird
☐ Brown Thrasher*
☐ Sage Thrasher
☐ Northern Mockingbird

Sturnidae: Starlings

☐ European Starling

Bombycillidae: Waxwings

☐ Bohemian Waxwing
☐ Cedar Waxwing

Ptilogonatidae: Silky Flycatchers

☐ Phainopepla*

Prunellidae: Accentors

☐ Siberian Accentor*

Passeridae: Sparrows

☐ House Sparrow

Motacillidae: Wagtails & Pipits

☐ Eastern Yellow Wagtail*
☐ Gray Wagtail*
☐ White Wagtail*
☐ Red-throated Pipit*
☐ American Pipit

Fringillidae: Finches

☐ Brambling*
☐ Evening Grosbeak
☐ Pine Grosbeak
☐ Gray-crowned Rosy-Finch
☐ House Finch
☐ Purple Finch
☐ Cassin's Finch
☐ Common Redpoll
☐ Hoary Redpoll*
☐ Red Crossbill
☐ White-winged Crossbill
☐ Pine Siskin
☐ Lesser Goldfinch
☐ Lawrence's Goldfinch*
☐ American Goldfinch

Calcariidae: Longspurs & Snow Buntings

☐ Lapland Longspur
☐ Chestnut-collared Longspur*
☐ Smith's Longspur*
☐ McCown's Longspur*
☐ Snow Bunting
☐ McKay's Bunting*

Emberizidae: Buntings

☐ Little Bunting*
☐ Rustic Bunting*

Passerellidae: American Sparrows

☐ Grasshopper Sparrow
☐ Black-throated Sparrow*
☐ Lark Sparrow
☐ Lark Bunting*
☐ Chipping Sparrow
☐ Clay-colored Sparrow
☐ Field Sparrow*
☐ Brewer's Sparrow
☐ Fox Sparrow
☐ American Tree Sparrow
☐ Dark-eyed Junco
☐ White-crowned Sparrow
☐ Golden-crowned Sparrow
☐ Harris's Sparrow
☐ White-throated Sparrow
☐ Sagebrush Sparrow
☐ Vesper Sparrow
☐ LeConte's Sparrow*
☐ Nelson's Sparrow*
☐ Savannah Sparrow
☐ Song Sparrow
☐ Lincoln's Sparrow
☐ Swamp Sparrow
☐ Green-tailed Towhee
☐ Spotted Towhee

Icteriidae: Yellow-breasted Chat

☐ Yellow-breasted Chat

Icteridae: Blackbirds and Orioles

☐ Yellow-headed Blackbird
☐ Bobolink
☐ Eastern Meadowlark*
☐ Western Meadowlark
☐ Orchard Oriole*
☐ Hooded Oriole*
☐ Bullock's Oriole

☐ Baltimore Oriole*
☐ Scott's Oriole*
☐ Red-winged Blackbird
☐ Tricolored Blackbird
☐ Brown-headed Cowbird
☐ Rusty Blackbird
☐ Brewer's Blackbird
☐ Common Grackle*
☐ Great-tailed Grackle*

Parulidae: Wood Warblers

☐ Ovenbird*
☐ Northern Waterthrush
☐ Golden-winged Warbler*
☐ Blue-winged Warbler*
☐ Black-and-white Warbler
☐ Prothonotary Warbler*
☐ Tennessee Warbler
☐ Orange-crowned Warbler
☐ Lucy's Warbler*
☐ Nashville Warbler
☐ MacGillivray's Warbler
☐ Mourning Warbler*
☐ Kentucky Warbler*
☐ Common Yellowthroat
☐ Hooded Warbler*
☐ American Redstart
☐ Cape May Warbler*
☐ Northern Parula*
☐ Magnolia Warbler*
☐ Bay-breasted Warbler*
☐ Blackburnian Warbler*
☐ Yellow Warbler
☐ Chestnut-sided Warbler
☐ Blackpoll Warbler*
☐ Black-throated Blue Warbler*
☐ Palm Warbler

☐ Yellow-rumped Warbler
☐ Yellow-throated Warbler*
☐ Prairie Warbler*
☐ Black-throated Gray Warbler
☐ Townsend's Warbler
☐ Hermit Warbler
☐ Black-throated Green Warbler*
☐ Canada Warbler*
☐ Wilson's Warbler
☐ Painted Redstart*

Cardinalidae: Cardinal and Grosbeaks

☐ Summer Tanager*
☐ Western Tanager
☐ Rose-breasted Grosbeak
☐ Black-headed Grosbeak
☐ Blue Grosbeak*
☐ Lazuli Bunting
☐ Indigo Bunting*
☐ Painted Bunting*
☐ Dickcissel*

Species Index

A

Acanthis flammea, 274
Accipiter
    cooperii, 162
    gentilis, 161
    striatus, 163
Actitis macularius, 105
Aechmophorus
    clarkii, 57
    occidentalis, 56
Aegolius
    acadicus, 185
    funereus, 184
Aeronautes saxatilis, 66
Agelaius
    phoeniceus, 306
    tricolor, 305
Aix sponsa, 10
Albatross, Black-footed, 142
Alectoris chukar, 40
Ammodramus savannarum, 291
Anas
    acuta, 18
    crecca, 19
    platyrhynchos, 17
Anser
    albifrons, 3
    caerulescens, 2
Anthus rubescens, 267
Antigone canadensis, 74
Aphelocoma californica, 222
Aquila chrysaetos, 159
Archilochus alexandri, 67
Ardea
    alba, 154
    herodias, 153
Ardenna grisea, 143

Arenaria
    interpres, 87
    melanocephala, 88
Artemisiospiza nevadensis, 289
Asio
    flammeus, 183
    otus, 182
Athene cunicularia, 178
Auklet
    Cassin's, 119
    Rhinoceros, 120
Avocet, American, 76
Aythya
    affinis, 22
    americana, 21
    collaris, 24
    marila, 23
    valisineria, 20

B

Bittern, American, 152
Blackbird
    Brewer's, 310
    Red-winged, 306
    Tricolored, 305
    Yellow-headed, 301
Bluebird
    Mountain, 255
    Western, 254
Bobolink, 302
Bombycilla
    cedrorum, 265
    garrulus, 264
Bonasa umbellus, 44
Botaurus lentiginosus, 152
Brachyramphus marmoratus, 117
Brant, 4

Branta
    bernicla, 4
    canadensis, 6
    hutchinsii, 5
Bubo
    scandiacus, 176
    virginianus, 175
Bucephala
    albeola, 32
    clangula, 30
    islandica, 31
Bufflehead, 32
Bunting
    Lazuli, 326
    Snow, 281
Bushtit, 239
Buteo
    jamaicensis, 168
    lagopus, 170
    regalis, 171
    swainsoni, 166
Butorides virescens, 155

C

Calcarius lapponicus, 280
Calidris
    alba, 91
    bairdii, 93
    canutus, 90
    mauri, 98
    melanotos, 96
    minutilla, 94
    ptilocnemis, 92
    pusilla, 97
    virgata, 89
Callipepla californica, 39
Calypte anna, 68
Canvasback, 20
Cardellina pusilla, 323
Cathartes aura, 157
Catharus
    fuscescens, 256
    guttatus, 258
    ustulatus, 257

Catherpes mexicanus, 245
Centrocercus urophasianus, 43
Cepphus columba, 116
Cerorhinca monocerata, 120
Certhia americana, 243
Chaetura vauxi, 65
Charadrius
    nivosus, 81
    semipalmatus, 82
    vociferus, 83
Chat, Yellow-breasted, 300
Chickadee
    Black-capped, 235
    Boreal, 238
    Chestnut-backed, 237
    Mountain, 236
Chlidonias niger, 138
Chondestes grammacus, 288
Chordeiles minor, 62
Chroicocephalus philadelphia, 124
Chukar, 40
Cinclus mexicanus, 250
Circus hudsonius, 160
Cistothorus palustris, 248
Clangula hyemalis, 29
Coccothraustes vespertinus, 268
Colaptes auratus, 197
Columba livia, 58
Contopus
    cooperi, 206
    sordidulus, 207
Coot, American, 71
Cormorant
    Brandt's, 149
    Double-crested, 148
    Pelagic, 147
Corvus
    brachyrhynchos, 225
    corax, 224
Cowbird, Brown-headed, 308
Crane, Sandhill, 74
Creeper, Brown, 243

Crossbill
    Red, 275
    White-winged, 276
Crow, American, 225
Curlew, Long-billed, 85
Cyanocitta stelleri, 223
Cygnus
    buccinator, 8
    columbianus, 9
Cypseloides niger, 64

D

Dendragapus
    fuliginosus, 48
    obscurus, 49
Dipper, American, 250
Dolichonyx oryzivorus, 302
Dove
    Eurasian Collared-, 60
    Mourning, 61
Dowitcher
    Long-billed, 101
    Short-billed, 100
Dryobates
    albolarvatus, 196
    pubescens, 194
    villosus, 195
    pileatus, 198
Duck
    Harlequin, 25
    Long-tailed, 29
    Ring-necked, 24
    Ruddy, 36
    Wood, 10
Dumetella carolinensis, 261

E

Eagle
    Bald, 164
    Golden, 159
Egret, Great, 154
Empidonax
    difficilis, 212
    hammondii, 209
    oberholseri, 211
    traillii, 208
    wrightii, 210
Eremophila alpestris, 227
Euphagus cyanocephalus, 310

F

Falcipennis canadensis, 45
Falco
    columbarius, 200
    mexicanus, 202
    peregrinus, 201
    sparverius, 199
Falcon
    Peregrine, 201
    Prairie, 202
Finch
    Cassin's, 273
    Gray-crowned Rosy-, 270
    House, 271
    Purple, 272
Flicker, Northern, 197
Flycatcher
    Ash-throated, 203
    Dusky, 211
    Gray, 210
    Hammond's, 209
    Olive-sided, 206
    Pacific-slope, 212
    Willow, 208
Fratercula cirrhata, 121
Fulica americana, 71
Fulmar, Northern, 146
Fulmarus glacialis, 146

G

Gadwall, 16
Gallinago delicata, 102
Gavia
    immer, 140
    pacifica, 141
    stellata, 139

Geothlypis
> *tolmiei,* 314
> *trichas,* 315
Glaucidium gnoma, 177
Godwit, Marbled, 86
Goldeneye
> Barrow's, 31
> Common, 30
Goldfinch
> American, 279
> Lesser, 278
Goose
> Cackling, 5
> Greater White-fronted, 3
> Snow, 2
Goshawk, Northern, 161
Grebe
> Clark's, 57
> Eared, 52
> Horned, 53
> Pied-billed, 55
> Red-necked, 54
> Western, 56
Grosbeak
> Black-headed, 325
> Evening, 268
> Pine, 269
Grouse
> Dusky, 49
> Greater Sage-, 43
> Ruffed, 44
> Sharp-tailed, 50
> Sooty, 48
> Spruce, 45
Guillemot, Pigeon, 116
Gull
> Bonaparte's, 124
> California, 129
> Glaucous-winged, 132
> Heermann's, 125
> Herring, 130
> Iceland, 131
> Mew, 126

Ring-billed, 127
Sabine's, 123
Western, 128

H

Haematopus bachmani, 75
Haemorhous
> *cassinii,* 273
> *mexicanus,* 271
> *purpureus,* 272
Haliaeetus leucocephalus, 164
Harrier, Northern, 160
Hawk
> Cooper's, 162
> Ferruginous, 171
> Red-tailed, 168
> Rough-legged, 170
> Sharp-shinned, 163
> Swainson's, 166
Heron
> Black-crowned Night-, 156
> Great Blue, 153
> Green, 155
Himantopus mexicanus, 77
Hirundo rustica, 233
Histrionicus histrionicus, 25
Hummingbird
> Anna's, 68
> Black-chinned, 67
> Calliope, 70
> Rufous, 69
Hydrobates
> *furcatus,* 145
> *leucorhous,* 144
Hydroprogne caspia, 134

I

Icteria virens, 300
Icterus bullockii, 304
Ixoreus naevius, 260

J

Jaeger
 Long-tailed, 114
 Parasitic, 113
 Pomarine, 112
Jay
 California Scrub-, 222
 Canada, 220
 Steller's, 223
Junco hyemalis, 298
Junco, Dark-eyed, 298

K

Kestrel, American, 199
Killdeer, 83
Kingbird
 Eastern, 205
 Western, 204
Kingfisher, Belted, 186
Kinglet
 Golden-crowned, 251
 Ruby-crowned, 252
Kittiwake, Black-legged, 122
Knot, Red, 90

L

Lagopus leucurus, 46
Lanius
 borealis, 215
 ludovicianus, 214
Lark, Horned, 227
Larus
 argentatus, 130
 californicus, 129
 canus, 126
 delawarensis, 127
 glaucescens, 132
 glaucoides, 131
 heermanni, 125
 occidentalis, 128

Leiothlypis
 celata, 312
 ruficapilla, 313
Leucosticte tephrocotis, 270
Limnodromus
 griseus, 100
 scolopaceus, 101
Limosa fedoa, 86
Longspur, Lapland, 280
Loon
 Common, 140
 Pacific, 141
 Red-throated, 139
Lophodytes cucullatus, 33
Loxia
 curvirostra, 275
 leucoptera, 276

M

Magpie, Black-billed, 226
Mallard, 17
Mareca
 americana, 14
 penelope, 15
 strepera, 16
Martin, Purple, 234
Meadowlark, Western, 303
Megaceryle alcyon, 186
Megascops kennicottii, 174
Melanerpes
 formicivorus, 188
 lewis, 187
Melanitta
 americana, 28
 deglandi, 27
 perspicillata, 26
Meleagris gallopavo, 51
Melospiza
 lincolnii, 294
 melodia, 293
Merganser
 Common, 34
 Hooded, 33
 Red-breasted, 35

Mergus
> *merganser,* 34
> *serrator,* 35
Merlin, 200
Molothrus ater, 308
Murre, Common, 115
Murrelet
> Ancient, 118
> Marbled, 117
Myadestes townsendi, 253
Myiarchus cinerascens, 203

N

Nighthawk, Common, 62
Nucifraga columbiana, 221
Numenius
> *americanus,* 85
> *phaeopus,* 84
Nutcracker, Clark's, 221
Nuthatch
> Pygmy, 242
> Red-breasted, 240
> White-breasted, 241
Nycticorax nycticorax, 156

O

Oreortyx pictus, 38
Oreoscoptes montanus, 262
Oriole, Bullock's, 304
Osprey, 158
Owl
> Snowy, 176
> Barn, 172
> Barred, 180
> Boreal, 184
> Burrowing, 178
> Flammulated, 173
> Great Gray, 181
> Great Horned, 175
> Long-eared, 182
> Northern Pygmy-, 177
> Northern Saw-whet, 185
> Short-eared, 183

> Spotted, 179
> Western Screech-, 174
Oxyura jamaicensis, 36
Oystercatcher, Black, 75

P

Pandion haliaetus, 158
Parkesia noveboracensis, 311
Partridge, Gray, 41
Passer domesticus, 266
Passerculus sandwichensis,
> 290
Passerella iliaca, 292
Passerina amoena, 326
Patagioenas fasciata, 59
Pelecanus
> *erythrorhynchos,* 150
> *occidentalis,* 151
Pelican
> American White, 150
> Brown, 151
Perdix perdix, 41
Perisoreus canadensis, 220
Petrel
> Fork-tailed Storm-, 145
> Leach's Storm-, 144
Petrochelidon pyrrhonota, 232
Pewee, Western Wood-, 207
Phalacrocorax
> *auritus,* 148
> *pelagicus,* 147
> *penicillatus,* 149
Phalaenoptilus nuttallii, 63
Phalarope
> Red, 111
> Red-necked, 110
> Wilson's, 108
Phalaropus
> *fulicarius,* 111
> *lobatus,* 110
> *tricolor,* 108
Phasianus colchicus, 42
Pheasant, Ring-necked, 42

Pheucticus melanocephalus, 325
Phoebastria nigripes, 142
Phoebe, Say's, 213
Pica hudsonia, 226
Picoides
    arcticus, 193
    dorsalis, 192
Pigeon
    Band-tailed , 59
    Rock, 58
Pinicola enucleator, 269
Pintail, Northern, 18
Pipilo
    chlorurus, 282
    maculatus, 283
Pipit, American, 267
Piranga ludoviciana, 324
Plectrophenax nivalis, 281
Plover
    American Golden-, 79
    Black-bellied, 78
    Pacific Golden-, 80
    Semipalmated, 82
    Snowy, 81
Pluvialis
    dominica, 79
    fulva, 80
    squatarola, 78
Podiceps
    auritus, 53
    grisegena, 54
    nigricollis, 52
Podilymbus podiceps, 55
Poecile
    atricapillus, 235
    gambeli, 236
    hudsonicus, 238
    rufescens, 237
Pooecetes gramineus, 287
Poorwill, Common, 63
Porzana carolina, 72
Progne subis, 234
Psaltriparus minimus, 239

Psiloscops flammeolus, 173
Ptarmigan, White-tailed, 46
Ptychoramphus aleuticus, 119
Puffin, Tufted, 121

Q

Quail
    California, 39
    Mountain, 38

R

Rail, Virginia, 73
Rallus limicola, 73
Raven, Common, 224
Recurvirostra americana, 76
Redhead, 21
Redpoll, Common, 274
Redstart, American, 316
Regulus
    calendula, 252
    satrapa, 251
Riparia riparia, 230
Rissa tridactyla, 122
Robin, American, 259

S

Salpinctes obsoletus, 244
Sanderling, 91
Sandpiper
    Baird's, 93
    Least, 94
    Pectoral, 96
    Rock, 92
    Semipalmated, 97
    Solitary, 104
    Spotted, 105
    Western, 98
Sapsucker
    Red-breasted, 191
    Red-naped, 190
    Williamson's, 189
Sayornis saya, 213

Scaup
    Greater, 23
    Lesser, 22
Scoter
    Black, 28
    Surf, 26
    White-winged, 27
Selasphorus
    calliope, 70
    rufus, 69
Setophaga
    coronata, 318
    nigrescens, 320
    occidentalis, 322
    petechia, 317
    ruticilla, 316
    townsendi, 321
Shearwater, Sooty, 143
Shoveler, Northern, 11
Shrike
    Loggerhead, 214
    Northern, 215
Sialia
    currucoides, 255
    mexicana, 254
Siskin, Pine, 277
Sitta
    canadensis, 240
    carolinensis, 241
    pygmaea, 242
Snipe, Wilson's, 102
Solitaire, Townsend's, 253
Sora, 72
Sparrow
    American Tree, 284
    Brewer's, 286
    Chipping, 285
    Fox, 292
    Golden-crowned, 295
    Grasshopper, 291
    House, 266
    Lark, 288
    Lincoln's, 294

    Sagebrush, 289
    Savannah, 290
    Song, 293
    Vesper, 287
    White-crowned, 296
Spatula
    clypeata, 11
    cyanoptera, 12
    discors, 13
Sphyrapicus
    nuchalis, 190
    ruber, 191
    thyroideus, 189
Spinus
    pinus, 277
    psaltria, 278
    tristis, 279
Spizella
    breweri, 286
    passerina, 285
Spizelloides arborea, 284
Starling, European, 263
Stelgidopteryx serripennis,
    231
Stercorarius
    longicaudus, 114
    parasiticus, 113
    pomarinus, 112
Sterna
    forsteri, 137
    hirundo, 135
    paradisaea, 136
Stilt, Black-necked, 77
Streptopelia decaocto, 60
Strix
    nebulosa, 181
    occidentalis, 179
    varia, 180
Sturnella neglecta, 303
Sturnus vulgaris, 263
Surfbird, 89

Swallow
    Bank, 230
    Barn, 233
    Cliff, 232
    Northern Rough-winged, 231
    Tree, 229
    Violet-green, 228
Swan
    Trumpeter, 8
    Tundra, 9
Swift
    Black, 64
    Vaux's, 65
    White-throated, 66
Synthliboramphus antiquus, 118

T

Tachycineta
    bicolor, 229
    thalassina, 228
Tanager, Western, 324
Tattler, Wandering, 103
Teal
    Blue-winged, 13
    Cinnamon, 12
    Green-winged, 19
Tern
    Arctic, 136
    Black, 138
    Caspian, 134
    Common, 135
    Forster's, 137
Thrasher, Sage, 262
Thrush
    Hermit, 258
    Swainson's, 257
    Varied, 260
Thryomanes bewickii, 249
Towhee
    Green-tailed, 282
    Spotted, 283

Tringa
    flavipes, 106
    incana, 103
    melanoleuca, 107
    solitaria, 104
Troglodytes
    aedon, 246
    pacificus, 247
Turdus migratorius, 259
Turkey, Wild, 51
Turnstone
    Black, 88
    Ruddy, 87
Tympanuchus phasianellus, 50
Tyrannus
    tyrannus, 205
    verticalis, 204
Tyto alba, 172

U

Uria aalge, 115

V

Veery, 256
Vireo
    cassinii, 217
    gilvus, 218
    huttoni, 216
    olivaceus, 219
Vireo
    Cassin's, 217
    Hutton's, 216
    Red-eyed, 219
    Warbling, 218
Vulture, Turkey, 157

W

Warbler
    Black-throated Gray, 320
    Hermit, 322
    MacGillivray's, 314
    Nashville, 313

Orange-crowned, 312
Townsend's, 321
Wilson's, 323
Yellow, 317
Yellow-rumped, 318
Waterthrush, Northern, 311
Waxwing
Bohemian, 264
Cedar, 265
Whimbrel, 84
Wigeon
American, 14
Eurasian, 15
Woodpecker
Acorn, 188
American Three-toed, 192
Black-backed, 193
Downy, 194
Hairy, 195
Lewis's, 187
Pileated, 198
White-headed, 196
Wren
Bewick's, 249
Canyon, 245
House, 246
Marsh, 248
Pacific, 247
Rock, 244

X

Xanthocephalus xanthocephalus, 301
Xema sabini, 123

Y

Yellowlegs
Greater, 107
Lesser, 106
Yellowthroat, Common, 315

Z

Zenaida macroura, 61
Zonotrichia
atricapilla , 295
leucophrys, 296

THE AMERICAN BIRDING ASSOCIATION STATE FIELD GUIDE SERIES

ARIZONA
ISBN 978-1-935622-60-4

CALIFORNIA
ISBN 978-1-935622-50-5

CAROLINAS
ISBN 978-1-935622-63-5

COLORADO
ISBN 978-1-935622-43-7

FLORIDA
ISBN 978-1-935622-48-2

HAWAIʻI
ISBN 978-1-935622-71-0

ILLINOIS
ISBN 978-1-935622-62-8

MASSACHUSETTS
ISBN 978-1-935622-66-6

MICHIGAN
ISBN 978-1-935622-67-3

MINNESOTA
ISBN 978-1-935622-59-8

NEW JERSEY
ISBN 978-1-935622-42-0

NEW YORK
ISBN 978-1-935622-51-2

OHIO
ISBN 978-1-935622-70-3

OREGON
ISBN 978-1-935622-68-0

PENNSYLVANIA
ISBN 978-1-935622-52-9

TEXAS
ISBN 978-1-935622-53-6

WASHINGTON
ISBN 978-1-935622-72-7

WISCONSIN
ISBN 978-1-935622-69-7

Dennis Paulson has taught university and adult-education courses about natural history for fifty-two years while living in Seattle. His last position was as the Director of the Slater Museum of Natural History at the University of Puget Sound. Dennis has written over ninety scientific papers and ten books, including *Birds of Puget Sound: Coast to Cascades*, *Shorebirds of the Pacific Northwest*, and *Shorebirds of North America: The Photographic Guide*. He has traveled on all the continents to observe and photograph birds and is also a world dragonfly expert.

Brian E. Small is a full-time professional bird and nature photographer. For more than thirty years, he has traveled widely across North America to capture images of birds in their native habitats. He served as the photo editor at *Birding* magazine for fifteen years. Small grew up in Los Angeles, graduated from U.C.L.A. in 1982, and still lives there today with his wife Ana, daughter Nicole, and son Tyler.

Quick Index

See the Species Index for a complete listing of all the birds in the *American Birding Association Field Guide to Birds of Washington*.

Albatross, 142
Auklet, 119–120
Avocet, 76
Bittern, 152
Blackbirds, 301, 305–306, 310
Bluebirds, 254–255
Bobolink, 302
Brant, 4
Bufflehead, 32
Buntings, 281, 326
Bushtit, 239
Canvasback, 20
Chat, 300
Chickadees, 235–238
Chukar, 40
Coot, 71
Cormorants, 147–149
Cowbird, 308
Crane, 74
Creeper, 243
Crossbills, 275–276
Crow, 225
Curlew, 85
Dipper, 250
Doves, 60–61
Dowitchers, 100–101
Ducks, 10–39
Eagles, 159–164
Egret, 154
Falcons, 201–202
Finches, 270–273
Flicker, 197
Flycatchers, 203–212
Fulmar, 146
Gadwall, 16
Godwit, 86
Goldeneyes, 30–31
Goldfinches, 278–279
Geese, 2–5
Goshawk, 161
Grebes, 52–57
Grosbeaks, 268–269, 325
Grouse, 43–45, 48–50
Guillemot, 116
Gulls, 123–132
Harrier, 160
Hawks, 162–163, 166–171
Herons, 153–156

Hummingbirds, 67–70
Jaeger, 112–114
Jays, 220, 222–223
Junco, 298
Kestrel, American, 199
Killdeer, 83
Kingbirds, 204–205
Kingfisher, 186
Kinglets, 251–252
Kittiwake, 122
Knot, 90
Lark, 227
Longspur, 280
Loons, 139–141
Magpie, 226
Mallard, 17
Martin, 234
Meadowlark, 303
Mergansers, 33–35
Merlin, 200
Murre, 115
Murrelets, 117–118
Nighthawk, 62
Nutcracker, 221
Nuthatches, 240–242
Oriole, 304
Osprey, 158
Owls, 172–185
Oystercatcher, 75
Partridge, 41
Pelicans, 150–151
Petrels, 144–145
Pewee, 207
Phalaropes, 108–110
Pheasant, 42
Phoebe, 213
Pigeons, 58–59
Pintail, 18
Pipit, 267
Plovers, 78–82
Poorwill, 63
Ptarmigan, 46
Puffin, 121
Quails, 38–39
Rail, 73
Raven, 224
Redhead, 21
Redpoll, 274
Redstart, 316

Robin, 259
Sanderling, 91
Sandpipers, 93–99, 104–105
Sapsuckers, 189–191
Scaup, 22–23
Scoters, 26–28
Shearwater, 143
Shoveler, 11
Shrikes, 214–215
Siskin, 277
Snipe, 102
Solitaire, 253
Sora, 72
Sparrows, 284–299
Starling, 263
Stilt, 77
Surfbird, 89
Swallows, 228–233
Swans, 8–9
Swifts, 64–66
Tanager, 324
Tattler, 103
Teal, 12–13, 19
Terns, 134–138
Thrasher, 262
Thrush, 257–258, 260
Towhee, 282–283
Turkey, 51
Turnstones, 87–88
Veery, 256
Vireo, 216–219
Vulture, 157
Warblers, 312–314, 317–323
Waterthrush, 311
Waxwings, 264–265
Whimbrel, 84
Wigeons, 14–15
Woodpeckers, 187–188, 192–198
Wrens, 244–249
Yellowlegs, 106–107
Yellowthroat, 315